More SEWING TO SELL

Take Your Handmade Business to the Next Level

16 New Projects to Make & Sell!

Virginia Lindsay

stash BOOKS

an imprint of C&T Publishing

Publisher: Amy Marson

Creative Director: Gailen Runge

Acquisitions Editor: Roxane Cerda

Managing Editor: Liz Aneloski

Editor: Lynn Koolish

Technical Editor: Julie Waldman

Cover/Book Designer: April Mostek

Production Coordinator: Tim Manibusan

Production Editor: Alice Mace Nakanishi

Illustrator: Valyrie Gillum

Photo Assistants: Mai Yong Vang and Michael Gardner

Cover photography by Lucy Glover of C&T Publishing, Inc.

Style photography by Lucy Glover and subjects photography
by Mai Yong Vang of C&T Publishing, Inc., unless otherwise noted

Published by Stash Books, an imprint of C&T Publishing, Inc., P.O. Box 1456,
Lafayette, CA 94549

Library of Congress Cataloging-in-Publication Data

Names: Lindsay, Virginia Keleher, 1975- author.

Title: More sewing to sell : take your handmade business to the next level :
16 new projects to make & sell! / Virginia Lindsay.

Description: Lafayette, California : Stash Books/C&T Publishing, [2018] |
Includes bibliographical references and index.

Identifiers: LCCN 2018009363 | ISBN 9781617454769 (soft cover : alk. paper)

Subjects: LCSH: Handicraft industries--Management--Handbooks, manuals,
etc. | Home-based businesses--Management--Handbooks, manuals, etc.
| Small business--Management--Handbooks, manuals, etc. | Selling--
Handbooks, manuals, etc.

Classification: LCC HD9999.H363 L56 2018 | DDC 746.068--dc23

LC record available at https://lccn.loc.gov/2018009363

Printed in China

10 9 8 7 6 5 4 3 2 1

Dedication

To Travis, for his patience, kindness, faith, and ability to see the best in everyone.
To Elsie, for her sense of style and wit.
To Anne, for her enthusiasm.
To Calvin, for his supportive nature.
To Marion, for bountiful hugs and kisses.

Acknowledgments

Thanks again to C&T Publishing for making this book possible; in particular, Roxane Cerda and Lynn Koolish. Many thanks to all the creative staff who made the book look gorgeous!

Thanks to my mom and dad for nurturing my creative spirit.

Thank you to Amy Frank, Anna Maria Horner, Lisa Jacobs, Kelly McCants, Kendra Oakden, Betsy Olmstead, Maryanne Petrus-Gilbert, and Amy Richardson-Golia. Your honest answers and shared information make this book a fabulous resource!

Thank you to Travis Lindsay for his advice about small business finances. It helps tremendously to have someone who tackles your business finances for you every year and then patiently explains why.

Thank you to all my friends and family who helped me with time management while writing this book!

CONTENTS

INTRODUCTION

I have been so pleased with all the wonderful feedback from my first book, *Sewing to Sell— The Beginner's Guide to Starting a Craft Business* (by Stash Books; see Resources, page 126). (For simplicity, I'll be referring to it from now on as *Sewing to Sell*.) Comments such as "This is going to help me so much!" and "I love the advice and projects to get my business started on the right foot!" have really carved a place in my heart for helping sewing entrepreneurs make their business dreams a reality. Being able to visit this topic again to provide even more detailed information on the business side of sewing is a privilege.

When you are involved daily in the process of keeping your handmade business afloat, you often forget that you need to continue to focus, refine, and expand your business. I often find myself so bogged down in the details of everyday maintenance—returning emails, preparing fabrics, checking supplies, and running promotions, that I sometimes forget to look at the overall health of my creative business. Am I working efficiently? Do I seek out new opportunities for sales? Am I wasting time on tasks that are not earning me enough income?

As it turns out, while writing, researching and interviewing for this book, I realized that even though I am an experienced and successful creative entrepreneur, I could do better! I do know how to market, buy smart, and organize my finances. I do know how to seek out new customers, nurture repeat customers, and create eye-catching promotions. But I also came to understand that even people with years of experience need a boost, training, a constant learning of new things, and an evaluation of their business plan. I want my sewing business to be the best it can possibly be, just like you do.

So, let's take this journey together. I will share what I know, what I have learned through extensive research, and we will all learn from the wisdom of some extremely talented women who are killing it in the sewing business—all from their own ideas and hard work. But, do you know what? They have had a lot of help along the way and had to be brave and smart when things got tough. Even someone who seems to have it all under control is still working to make things better. Just as with all businesses, there is no fast formula for success in sewing for sales.

One particular quote that resonates with me is from an interview with Lisa Jacobs (page 32), my favorite marketing expert for creative people such as us. Lisa says:

> *"The biggest mistake I see new creatives making is overestimating other online businesses and underestimating themselves. I feel like a lot of my success can be attributed to my 'If they can do it, I can do it' attitude."*

I love that! We can all do it! Stop comparing and own your success, no matter what level you feel you have achieved. Many people are still stuck in wishing they could start a sewing business, and you—yes, *you*—have already accomplished one of the hardest parts: You have begun and are willing to keep working hard to make it better.

So, if we stand in our own way by making busy work instead of moving forward, we may throw up our hands in frustration saying:

- Why won't they buy?

- Where are my customers?

- Why can't I figure out these numbers?

- I feel like I am working so hard but never making enough money!

- How can I keep doing this alone?

This book is going to answer those questions and many more that you never even thought to ask. And just as in *Sewing to Sell*, you'll see sixteen copyright-free projects to sew and sell. I encourage you to take these projects and make them your own. They are good foundations that you can make special by applying *your* talents. They are organized to make it easy for you to implement your own style of sewing. Perhaps you love to coordinate fabrics but don't want to get into tiny details; try the Big Boxy Patchwork Bag (page 76) and see how it inspires you. Or maybe you want to focus on spreading your love of handmade to the environmentally conscious by making the very handy Market Bag (page 122) from organic fabrics. Everyone can find at least one project they'd like to make.

I am so excited to share this book with you. I hope that you learn from this information and that your sewing business dreams come true. And, you must know that I, and all the crafty, kind, and wise businesswomen featured in this book, are rooting for you to make your business a true success.

Thank you, and happy sewing!

—*Virginia Lindsay*

SEARCHING OUT YOUR NICHE

What Is a Niche? How Do You Find Yours?

Simply put, a niche is a segment of a marketplace. A niche is where your special style and talents meet your audience and propel you into a successful small business. If only finding your niche was as easy as searching the internet for the definition, we would all be happily running our own small profitable businesses already.

As an individual, you know you can't compete with huge global companies making similar goods. Target and Pier 1 Imports are going to have the resources to make throw pillows cheaper and faster than you. Anthropologie is a huge chain of stores and can outsource global workers to hand macramé the most

beautiful scarf you can imagine. It can feel daunting, but the question you need to ask yourself is, "What can I do that my competition cannot?" The answer is how you begin to find your creative business niche. A niche market doesn't compete with a big factory and a niche business person doesn't sell to millions of people. But, a niche can support you (and maybe even a few employees) happily and profitably.

Now for the question, *how do you find your niche?* To be honest, it's a journey and it takes work. Here are some helpful steps to help you craft your own niche and start your journey.

STEP 1: FOLLOW YOUR PASSION

Focus on what you *love* to make. Let's assume you have been running your sewing business for some time and sewing a variety of things. Even though that hand-embroidered basket sells, if you hate the detail work—stop making it! Your lack of passion is going to be the first roadblock and it is going to prevent you from being a success.

Keep trying new things to sew until you find the thing (or things) that not only sells, but that you love to make. Yes, sometimes the grind of cut, sew, and repeat can get you down, but if you step back and still love your handmade items, then you know it is a prize.

Incorporate your talents into creating something that you know people will love.

Photo by Virginia Lindsay

We all have our own talents and gifts. Your passions are going to help you to head in the right direction. But for now, you have to use practical knowledge to find something other people feel passionate about too. For example, you know that you love sewing patchwork and you have a talent for combining fabrics. Now comes the question, *what should you make with the patchwork?*

I have sold hundreds of these Crayon Art Folios. They are cute, useful, washable, and make fantastic gifts. I don't always love sewing them over and over again, but I delight in the excited faces of kids and moms who see their fun and potential, making this product a staple of my shop.

STEP 2: IDENTIFY YOUR CUSTOMER

Think about who you want to be in business with. Not just women. Not just kids or moms. But narrow your criteria down to kids who love to draw. Or maybe think about artsy older women who love to travel around the world. Or perhaps you want to sell to mothers of toddlers who love organic handmade baby gear.

When you have identified the person, make a list of what they would like and what would be useful to them. Putting them first will give you a special advantage for creating something they will love. Let's take the older woman for example.

For the artsy older woman who loves to travel:

- Totes with pockets and zippers to close
- Cross-body bag for essentials/passport
- Organizers to bring home postcards/small souvenirs
- Travel journal
- Colorful patchwork
- Bold colors
- Washable

A niche can be born from sewing for your own family. Creating fun, colorful, yet natural style for kids is the niche for my own sewing. These bags were a seasonal offering I made in the fall of 2016.

Then, think about what makes *you* the special person to connect with this specific person. Are you someone who loves to travel too? Or have you been making gifts for your own artsy mom and her friends when they go on their trips? How are you specifically qualified to create something that will be special and useful to this certain person? You have to like and identify with this person in order to create for them.

STEP 3: DO YOUR RESEARCH

Now you know what you love to make and whom you want to make it for. *Business is a two-way street, and most of the traffic goes toward your customer because they are doing the purchasing.* You have to create a product that people want and need. You can't be everything to everyone, but you can be something special to someone who needs the special something that you make. Think hard about this person and how your handmade products can make their life better. This gives you a thoughtful connection that will shine through in your sewing. Most likely you will either be one of these people yourself or have good knowledge of people like this.

Make yourself an inspiration board, clip magazines, make Pinterest boards (pinterest.com), flip through catalogs, go through your favorite websites, follow artists you admire, study organizations you care about, question your friends, and gather information. This step can go on and on for some people, so give yourself a time frame here—a few weeks or a month at the most before you head on to the next step.

STEP 4: MAKE SAMPLES

By now, what you want to make should be starting to take shape. You have thought about your target audience and brainstormed, you have searched for inspiration, and you have some good ideas. You feel excited, passionate, and inspired. It's time to start sewing.

Be sure to use your talents here. If you are a superfast and efficient sewist, you can add extra detail while keeping your fabrics simple. If you have a knack for patchwork, make your pieces bright and colorful, but make sure you are keeping your work time reasonable by cutting down on detail (pockets, zippers, pleats, and so on). If you love working with special fabrics, such as leather, go for it—but keep your customer in mind the whole time—am I spending so much on materials that I am going to price out my target customer?

After you have some things made, think again about the topics discussed above. Do you like making it and feel proud of it? Is your niche customer going to like and want this? Is this going to be something that you can price reasonably and still compensate yourself properly?

Photo by Amy Bader

Amy Frank (page 11) made Blessing Bands for her own children and as gifts for friends and family. The kids loved wearing them and felt excited about their messages. The parents loved having something so positive and special for their kids. She knew she had a great new product for her Mindfully Made Studios.

STEP 5: CONFIRM YOUR PRODUCTS

In other words, *are your items what you want to sell, and do you like making them?* After you have a few samples (and you are welcome to use the projects in this book to save yourself time and effort), it's time to test the products with family and friends and see what kind of reaction you get. Show your family and have them try them out. Use your social media channels. Maybe give a few away as gifts, offer them for sale as samples, or both. What kind of response do you get?

As a business person, think of finding your niche in terms of crafting. You have to make choices and decisions. You have to see what works best and what looks beautiful. All crafting is unique and business niches are unique too. Your niche should be a coming together of your special talents and your selected audience. You can do this!

Amy Frank of Mindfully Made Studios:
Finding Your Niche

Amy Frank has been a sewist since she started sewing with her mom in high school and dreamed of being a fashion designer. Her first commercial sewing adventure was as a young mom when she started Amy Frank Handbags. After having her second child, Amy took a break from the business and in the next few years had two more children and concentrated on being a mom. Now a mother of four, Amy has created her second sewing business— Mindfully Made Studios. This time around, Amy carefully crafted a business plan that fits into a niche by focusing in on her best-selling handmade product, Blessing Bands. Amy also runs The Makery in downtown State College, Pennsylvania, a gorgeous and creative space for art and craft classes.

What made you decide to start Mindfully Made Studios?

After I had my four children, I wanted to create and sell work again, but I had conditions: I wanted that work to be both meaningful and scalable. I wanted my work to make a difference to the people who wore it, and I wanted to create something that could be produced on a larger scale than my custom handbags but was still handmade.

Who is your ideal customer? How do you connect with this person through Mindfully Made Studios?

I like to think that our Blessing Bands connect our customers to peace, presence, and purpose, helping them to be stronger and more mindful in their daily lives. Our ideal customer is a woman, typically a mom, between 25 and 55, who wants to live a more inspired life.

Photo by Amy Bader

Mindfully Made Studios targets women who want to be more present and in touch with their spirituality. A handmade yoga mat carrier is perfect for this type of customer.

What inspired you to start making Blessing Bands?

I had just had my fourth child in five years and was feeling really lost creatively and personally—all those overwhelmed feelings that young moms often experience. I wanted something bright and bold, but attractive to wear that would instantly remind me of how blessed I was, and would also be like a secret power I could draw on when I needed strength. The focus word on the exterior of the bracelet was the reminder and the interior passage felt like wearing a hidden superpower—a little extra inspiration.

I made a few for myself and one for a good friend who was going through a hard time. Other friends noticed them and it grew from there.

I think the Blessing Band is so smart and creative. What made you decide to focus on it as your main product?

After selling a few to friends and then at local art shows, I realized they were very meaningful and helpful to people in their daily lives. I also realized that they were simple enough to be scalable. These two traits made them a perfect focus for my company.

Photo by Amy Bader

Amy continues to work to make her product more stylish and modern for her customers. In the spring of 2017, she introduced a new line of metal- and leather-plated styles.

What do you see as the future of Mindfully Made Studios?

I will continue to create Blessing Bands—we just recently came out with metal- and leather-plated styles. I would also like to move into a few other product lines that continue our mission of bringing peace, presence, and purpose.

Thank you so much to Amy Frank for sharing her story of the Blessing Band and finding her niche in a busy marketplace. We can certainly learn a great deal from Amy's planning and observations to find our own niche business!

Visit Amy online: mindfullymadestudios.com • themakerypa.com

FOCUSING AND FINE-TUNING YOUR SHOP—ONLINE AND ON THE ROAD

Your shop has been up and running for a while and things are going pretty well. But you are starting to feel like you are ready to up your game so that your handmade business takes off and brings you the kind of independence and income you have been dreaming of. It is time to give your shop a boost by approaching your fundamentals with a fresh eye and a new look.

To look at your shop with fresh eyes, take a moment to bring to life your ideal customer. What would she see? Your ideal shopper is the person you are making the product for. (You'll learn more about her in Identifying Your Customer, page 29.) Imagine her as a real person—is she a busy mom and you are making her life easier with your trendy spacious totes? Does she love to work out and you are helping her to look great with your fantastic workout headbands? What will this person see when she visits your shop? What can you do to keep her on your website long enough to make a purchase and become a repeat customer?

NOTE

Most people running a sewing business have an online shop. If you do not have an online presence, you must take the plunge! Even if you prefer to generate sales in person at shows, customers expect to be able to find you online. At its most basic, take photos of the things you sell and describe them in a ready-made online shop format, such as Big Cartel, Shopify, or Etsy. (For more information about places to set up shop online, check out the Selling chapter in my book *Sewing to Sell*, page 127.)

Photography

You only have a few seconds to grab a customer's attention, so bright, beautiful, descriptive photos are a *must*. You cannot get away with unprofessional photos if you want to move up to the next level of business. You need to either hire someone or get some training yourself to learn how to use a DSLR (digital single-lens reflex) camera (see Resources, Photography, page 126).

PRODUCT PHOTOS

Most online shop owners do a combination of photographing their basic product themselves and hiring someone to show their products in action. This way, you can change fabrics or colors, but use that gorgeous professional photography repeatedly in your online shop.

What should those basic photos look like? They need to have a neutral backdrop so that nothing in the background is distracting and your customer can see the details. The photos should show the item at different angles and be descriptive. That is, the photos should show the special features as if your ideal customer is able to pick up the item and look at it herself. For example, if you are photographing the adorable llama and you have six photos (Etsy now allows up to ten photos) to share, show the whole animal, the side, the back, and a detail of the face so they can see how well-made the item is. The last photo should show the product in action—in this case being cuddled by a child.

Your job is to learn the ins and outs of taking those first six to nine shots. You can set this up in your basement (or any normally dark room) workshop by purchasing good lights, using a simple backdrop, and learning how to use your nice camera.

Photos by Virginia Lindsay

Your home product photo studio doesn't need to be fancy. For small products, you can use a setting such as this. The key is good lighting and knowing the proper settings on your DSLR camera. And if you do not have the photography eye for these shots, hire someone who does have the talent.

What about the engaging photo with the cute child? You have gotten this far and you must know someone who has the setting you are looking for if it is not in your own home or yard! Hire a professional and get some gorgeous shots in this perfect setting! This investment will be repaid many times over in sales.

In order to really have a successful online shop, your photography must be the very best it can be.

Photos by Virginia Lindsay

This front photo with entire item in the photo would traditionally be the main photo.

This side shot shows one side of the item.

This detail shot shows the back.

This descriptive photo shows the yarn hair and gives an idea of the top.

A close up detail is always helpful.

This product photo shows a cute kid holding the item. It gives a good idea of the size and helps customers imagine how the item will be loved at their own home.

Product and Marketing Copy

The next most important element is describing your product. This is called writing sales copy (also known as *copy writing*). These little descriptive paragraphs are the bones of your sales strategy. Again, consider investing in training to really learn the best methods for selling your precious handmade products. You may have something perfect for your ideal customer, but if they can't understand what they are buying, all those perfect photos will be for nothing (see the complete copy-writing course by Lisa Jacobs under Marketing Resources, page 32)!

A very useful copy tip includes helping your customers imagine using your product. If you are describing a quilt, let them know how cozy it will feel. Tell them it is be treasured by their family for generations. Tell them about the special design and its traditions. You can write very briefly about your involvement, but don't focus too much on yourself. You can write a separate story about your process on your blog and give them a link if they want to know about that (and this is great to share on social media).

But most people want to imagine only themselves when it comes to making a purchase. You must appeal to their needs to compel them to purchase.

Photo by Kendra Oakden

Kendra Oakden of Swankaroo (page 38) describes her product as not only helping ease the work for mom by encouraging kids to carry their own stuff, but she also appeals to the emotions of savoring childhood and encouraging creativity.

TITLES

It's good to consider a few things when writing sales descriptions for the web. First, understand that the vast majority of people scan quickly instead of carefully reading online. They are browsing, and it's important that you grab their attention quickly. You can do this with catchy descriptive titles, such as "Chic Poolside Water-Resistant Tote" instead of "Large Bag." The title can be clever but it must also be descriptive.

Examples:

- Cross-Body Denim Zipper Purse for Travelers, *rather than* Zippy Bag

- Reusable Organic Cotton Market Tote, *rather than* Cloth Grocery Bag

- Patchwork Scrappy Handmade Quilted Baby Pillow, *rather than* Scrap Pillow

PRODUCT DESCRIPTION

After you draw them in with the title, use short descriptive paragraphs, bullets, and lists, making it easy for your readers to see what it is you are creating and how it can benefit them. Make sure they know that you are creating a solution to a problem they have—a fashion problem, an organization problem, a gift-giving problem, a decor problem, a workout problem.

Give the basics of size and materials, but there is no need to go into extra detail unless this is something that is very personalized. They are more interested in seeing themselves using this product and how it will make their lives better.

If your customer has already gotten this far reading the description, they most likely are interested in your product. Now, you need to close the sale. How? By establishing trust and value to your product with simple, honest phrases. You are an expert sewer with an established business—let your potential customer know your value and the value of your handmade item. For example, "I am so excited to share this handmade clutch with you, and I know you will appreciate the high-quality materials and the fine craftsmanship that has gone into every single one of my pieces."

Another option is to hire a professional copywriter or take a copywriting course to perfect your skills. It's always a good idea to have someone with good writing skills proofread for grammar and spelling!

Show Booths—Taking It to the Professional Level

For those of you who prefer to sell in person, your booth and sales tactics are now ready for an upgrade. It is time to invest in your booth. Even if you have been getting by on makeshift, "shabby chic" booths, you will feel really inspired by these wise words by Kelly McCants.

SPOTLIGHT INTERVIEW

Kelly McCants of Modern June:
The Ins and Outs of Taking Your Show on the Road

Kelly McCants is the creator of Modern June, and has traveled the country setting up her booth at shows large and small. Kelly created her own brand and look using oilcloth and vintage apron styles. She has written two books, Sewing with Oil Cloth *(by Wiley Publishing)* and At Home with Modern June *(by Stash Books).*

What was your first show booth like and what did you learn from that experience?

My first venture was to sell vintage aprons and oilcloth totes at a farmers' market where I had a stall. Every booth had its own set of tiered shelves to use. At first, I just put my totes right on the wood shelves and tied the aprons on an inexpensive clothing rack.

A few weeks in I bought a mannequin to help display the aprons. Unfortunately, it was top-heavy and toppled over at the slightest touch. I only took it to the market once. I quickly learned that I could sell the apron that I was wearing. I became a model of sorts, picking the best apron to start off my show day.

I couldn't let go of the vintage aprons without making patterns from them. Quickly, I was combining patterns and creating my hand-made aprons out of cotton and oilcloth. Along with my handmade aprons, I started making wallets and coin purses out of the oil-cloth. That is when I began to use items from my kitchen as display pieces such as enamel-ware and vintage aluminum pots and pans.

My products and my display evolved that summer. I learned a lot from my fellow vendors. I spent a lot of time combing local

Inspired by vintage patterns, Kelly created bright functional bibs, smocks, and skirts that attracted customers to her booth.

gift shops and Flickr for inspiration for setting up my booth. Keep in mind, this was 2006—before Pinterest, blogs, and social media were just coming up in the world, so inspiration wasn't as easy to obtain as it is today.

What were some of the best improvements you made to your booth as you gained experience?

Within four years, I went from a tiny 3-×-4-foot market stall, to 6-foot tables at indie craft fairs, to expansive 10-×-20-foot booths at national shows around the country. After I had gone to my first Country Living Fair, I knew that I had to step up my game. My typical indie craft table set-up got lost in the vintage farmhouse feel of the surrounding booths.

In the end, I had as many props for my set-up as I had merchandise—so much so, that the following year I started renting trucks because I could no longer fit it all in my minivan. I found that setting the mood was essential to success. I created a homey kitchen like setting as best I could.

I quickly learned that hauling around real dinette tables and Hoosier cabinets was costly, in space and expenses. I opted to use small cupboards, lightweight bakers racks, and vintage shelves on top of regular folding tables covered with tablecloths to create the kitschy look that suited my wares.

The old cabinets and vintage shelves from the 1950s also helped me to gain height. No matter where you are selling, you need to take advantage of your vertical space. By doing so, you get to sell more merchandise. But, the real bonus is that you can attract the attention of those who can't see your booth through the crowd of happy customers surrounding your table. If they get a peek of your wares, the chances are good that they will be patient and wait to see more, thus increasing your sales.

Modern June's booth creates a homey, nostalgic atmosphere to help sell her product.

I used vintage suitcases, picnic baskets, and housewares to create a kitschy experience in my booth and to help me gain added height. I also packed my items in the containers and used them as storage at the show. Everything I take to show has to serve multiple purposes.

What were the advantages of getting a larger booth space?

I found that paying for a double booth not only gave me more room for my extended product line, it also gave me room for customers. When more people can get into the tent, it means more sales.

As a bonus, the location of this larger space got me out into an area that was far more visible. I was no longer in the middle of a sea of white tents. I never regretted paying extra for that exposure, I easily recouped my money and always profited from it.

A word of caution: I would not opt for an extralarge booth at a fair that I hadn't attended at least once. I like to get the lay of the land first and make sure that my products are a good fit before spending all that extra money. It's safer that way.

In preparing for a show on the road, what has your experience taught you? In your opinion, what separates a novice from a professional at a big show?

In my option, a professional sets themselves apart from a novice by being prepared.

Preparation is the key. In a perfect world, my team and I would be done crafting merchandise a week before leaving for a show. There are so many things that can help you achieve an easier load-in / setup day if you have the time to do so. I have found that the more stressful the setup, the harder it is for me to be a happy vendor. A happy seller always equals better show and increased sales.

A professional keeps lists and timelines, so they aren't recreating the wheel for each show. Now that doesn't mean that it's perfect or set in stone, my records are constantly being added to and tweaked. I use Google Docs for most of these to-do lists, that way my shop manager can help me stay on track during a busy show prep.

Do you have some tips for traveling to shows?

Tips for traveling to shows:

- Pack wares into display cabinets and props when possible. Doing so saves space and it speeds up your setup time.
- Use stretch wrap (commonly used to wrap shipping pallets, available where shipping supplies are sold) to keep the product on shelving units. Be sure to take your wrap to the show with you.
- Pack your van or truck with your product and display pieces first, tables second, and tents last. This way you can unload these items in opposite order at the show.
- Keep a box of thick trash bags for big soft items, such as pillows, and squish them into the middle of larger things to save space.

- Pack food and drinks. Don't count on being able to get anything to eat or drink at a show, especially on setup day. Always bring your own caffeine!

- Always carry a show kit—load up a small box with tape, hooks, tiny tools, travel size toiletries, pain relievers (such as ibuprofen, acetaminophen, cold meds), pens, phone chargers, cords, and more. Think about what you always need and what you always forget. Pack this kit after a show and don't rob it in between shows. You and your fellow vendors will thank you for it.

- When traveling to a new show, do your research. Look online to see pictures of past shows; social media is a great way to get the lay of the land and help you prepare your booth, load in, and ultimately ensure your success.

- Book your hotel as soon as you get accepted into a show. If you book directly with the hotel you don't have to prepay. I learned the hard way that rooms fill up quickly, and you don't want to get stuck in a hotel that is far from the show.

How do you present yourself and connect with customers in person? Do you have some tips for "closing the sale"?

I try to present myself as Modern June— a modern June Cleaver, friendly, warm, and knowable. Since I only sell items that I need and use it's easy to connect them to my life. I find that if I have a story behind why I use it, then my customers can see why they need it too.

It's most important to find your people, the people that connect with you and your wares.

They give you the will to go on because they get you and they believe in you. It takes time and a lot of trial and error and it often changes after a few years. I tried a variety of venues, farmers' markets, indie craft shows, and the larger national shows. I was amazed when I first realized that there were people out there to whom my brand resonated. From there, everything took off.

What is the one thing that would help you travel to shows if money was no object?

I dream of having a large cargo van. It needs to be extra tall and a really long. Not only would this help me get to out-of-town shows, I could use it to store all my show props, boxes, and tents.

Since we're talking fantasyland, I'd also like free and safe place to park the van too.

Thank you, Kelly! What wonderful descriptive advice to really get your booth up to date and looking professional.

Visit Kelly online: modernjuneblog.wordpress.com

ARE YOU READY TO EXPAND?

When do you know it's time to spend some of those profits and help your business grow? What if you realized that the biggest reason your business was not growing is because you were holding it back yourself? It's a rut many of us get into and it's a challenge to get out of it. This chapter will give you the facts about expanding your business and if it is really the right move for you.

The first question you have to ask yourself is can your business sustain expansion? Do you have more work than you can handle? Are you turning down jobs? If you answered *yes*, you are certainly ready. But even if you answered *no*, expansion might be what you need to really get your business going in the right direction.

You can explore the three main avenues for expanding your business: wholesale, manufacturing, and hiring employees.

Selling Wholesale

If one of the main things you need is exposure to customers, wholesale might be a great option for you. Having your handmade items in shops (actual storefronts and busy online shops) gives you lots of exposure that you don't have to go out and grab for yourself. This gives you time to actually make and lets you stop constantly promoting. The drawback? Shop owners need to be able to mark up their goods at least 40% to make a reasonable profit. Can you take that kind of hit on your bottom line? If you have created a line of handmade goods that translates into proper profit margins, the answer should be *yes*.

SPOTLIGHT INTERVIEW

Maryanne Petrus-Gilbert of Sardine Clothing Co.
Selling Wholesale

Here to tell us about her wholesale business is Maryanne Petrus-Gilbert of Sardine Clothing Company. She started her company in 2008 and has been creating gorgeous skirts and other clothing from recycled T-shirts ever since. She sells her unique line of handmade clothing in shops all over the United States.

Photos by Nick Pedersen

Maryanne Petrus-Gilbert (center) and helpers model her original clothing line made from upcycled T-shirts and sweaters.

What made you decide to start selling wholesale?

I actually started Sardine with the sole intention of only doing wholesale. I was a recent widow, mom of three kids, and the thought of getting on the road to sell shirts at art shows and festivals was not an option. I initially had my work in a few local stores and it was going well until I did a retail show.

Then quickly I was drawn in and let the wholesale pursuit fall to the wayside.

In the past three years though, I have been steadily moving back to a more wholesale-based business. I love being able to stay home and travel less.

How did you make connections with retailers?

Currently I have a few venues for meeting retailers. I exhibit twice a year at NY NOW. I set up again at ACRE (American Craft Retailers Expo). I also have online outlets with Etsy Wholesale and IndieMe. I love meeting retailers and discussing the best options for their particular store and when to have them start carrying my clothing. It is not good to just get an order, you really need to have a store that works with your line and will become a lifelong retailer. Sometimes I have to advise that Sardine might not be a good fit and that is okay too.

Maryanne is careful that her style fits with the store she is partnering with to sell her handmade clothing line. This creates a lasting and happy relationship between Sardine clothing company, the store, and the customer.

Do you find it hard to keep up with orders?

I spend at least eight hours every day in the studio. This is my full-time job and I am very committed to making it work. I produce work before it is actually ordered and then there is no need to stress about filling an order. Every new year I set myself improvement goals, and about five years ago it was to always be prepared for a show. The next year it was to be prepared for two shows, so the work I am making now is in theory not needed for anything in particular. It is a good feeling to be able to just make a few "fill in" pieces for a special order.

What particular advice would give someone who is interested in selling her handmade goods wholesale?

I think starting with a working wholesale price makes everything work out better. Many artists tend to start in retail and are unable to scale the pricing for wholesale.

Thank you so much to Maryanne for her honest and helpful advice about moving your business into the wholesale marketplace! I love the idea of starting out with a plan to be wholesale.

Visit Maryanne online: sardineclothing.com

Hiring Help

Knowing your strengths and your weaknesses is important. Hiring a helper, or several, can make your business more efficient and propel you to a new level of success. This sounds like an easy decision to make. So, what could possibly go wrong? The biggest risk in hiring is potentially losing some control of business decisions and possibly losing a level of quality that your customers have come to expect. You have to find the balance and hopefully come to understand what an asset employees can be to your handmade business.

SPOTLIGHT INTERVIEW

Anna Maria Horner of Craft South
Hiring Help for Your Business

Here to help and bring her years of experience and wisdom is Anna Maria Horner. Anna not only runs her own design brand, but also is the founder and proprietor of Nashville's Craft South. Anna's expertise and success in the sewing industry is due not only to her wonderful talent but also her business savvy and hard work.

Taking the step to hire help seems to be a big hurdle for many in creative businesses. When did you hire your first employee and what kind of a difference did it make in helping your business grow?

It is a big step and in my case it was way back when I had my first business at 23. I had opened a small dress shop where my mother and I were making all the clothes. It was only the two of us. If I was sewing, Mom was working the counter. If she was sewing, I was working the counter. If there was no one in the shop, which happened more frequently than it should have, then we were both sewing! We both had this natural, self-reliant tendency to think we could handle this sort of setup indefinitely. It honestly wasn't until people starting asking about employment in our shop, that I started thinking about getting help.

My first emotional response was "… they won't understand what I want." I feel almost embarrassed to admit that now, but I think, in retrospect, that emotion is very telling of being a creative head of business. It all feels so personal to us that we protect it. Ultimately, hiring someone in that situation just gave us a little breathing space and covered the practical situation of when we both needed to be away. But I was very conservative with how many shop hours I paid out to a staff member simply because of the revenue we were not yet making.

What was the process like to hire and train people in the early stages of building your career?

When I was beginning the format of business that I am still in to this day (designing textiles, designing and wholesaling a sewing pattern line, and running an online shop that sells both along with other product collection partnerships), I again felt I should manage it all myself.

But soon after I opened my online shop in December 2007, I found that I simply could not meet the deadlines of designing the product if I was also cutting and shipping all the orders. This predicament is a very good one. It meant that I was diversifying my revenue streams, which indicates growth. And while it feels like you are giving away money

in the beginning, what you are really doing is allowing yourself to concentrate on those parts you are meant for, which for me was the designing. At the same time, you are increasing the productivity potential of those parts that you don't have to do yourself, in my case the cutting and shipping of my fabrics. So it started with one part-time college student. The position grew into a full-time online sales and studio manager before hiring a second part-time fulfillment position.

With moving my online studio out of my house and opening Craft South, we now have about ten employees, so my design studio operates entirely from home alone now and separate from all the retail. It has remained important that for the most part, throughout the past decade, every job I have hired for, I have once occupied myself at some stage. So the training for the position in the beginning and what is required of it comes from my own experience. One of the most rewarding things about having a team is that each member has a special approach and perspective that a single person simply cannot. And beyond the hours devoted, there is so much value in having many minds contribute to a whole under your orchestration. Now watching each of my staff enhance each of their roles and then teach them to each other is especially rewarding.

Anna Maria Horner (*center*) with Elizabeth Thomas (*left*), who is the buyer and inventory manager, and Jennifer Reichert (*right*), who is the sales and staff manager at Craft South

Now that you have had staff for many years, what advice would you give someone just beginning this process?

Running a business with staff, like parenting a family with children, is an imperfect, humbling yet rewarding process. Allowing everyone room for mistakes and then making thoughtful correction is so important. Keeping the focus on the collective goals of the business, rather than on one personality or another in any given situation, is key to meaningful growth and success.

I find there has to be a balanced hand of nurturing both your staff and your business at the same time. When something unexpected or even very negative happens, don't forget that it is yet another opportunity to remind yourself of what it felt like to do it all alone and what you need to do to keep that heart of it alive, all the while persevering. Change is good for business, just like life, so don't be afraid of it.

Thank you so much, Anna! These wise words about letting go of some control while gaining a new perspective and business growth and truly appreciated.

Visit Anna Maria online: annamariahorner.com

Manufacturing

Getting help with production can be a real challenge. Do you want to hire a few people and set up shop in your home studio? Or do you want to actually outsource the production to a manufacturing company? This is a big step and worthy of a lot of investigation and planning. But professional equipment and large-scale production capabilities can be a huge benefit to your business. It takes hard work to find the right manufacturer and to make sure that quality is maintained. Are you up for the challenge?

Begin by looking at the several websites available to match your needs with a manufacturer. These sites claim to accept only reputable and established companies from overseas and in the United States. For overseas production, you can start with Bambify (bambify.com, recommended by Shopify and marks companies as start-up friendly). It is free to use. For USA-only production, Maker's Row (makersrow.com) is recommended, but it does have a membership

Amy Frank (page 11) has two workers who meet three times a week, and together with Amy, they produce Blessing Bands for Mindfully Made Studios.

fee. This service can match you with manufacturers and take some of the work and stress out of your search.

Doing your own research of local manufacturers is also an option. Make sure to visit the factory and check for cleanliness and organization. Ask for references and do your homework. Order samples and be very clear on your specifications. It is important to be prepared as much as possible when approaching a manufacturing partnership.

SPOTLIGHT INTERVIEW

Betsy Olmsted, Textile Designer
Finding a Manufacturer

Betsy Olmsted is a textile designer of gorgeous vivid watercolor fabrics. Her pieces include pillows, tea towels, table runners, aprons, and more. Her work has been featured in the magazines Country Living, House Beautiful, HGTV Magazine, *and the popular blog* Design*Sponge.

What led you to change your business plan from creating all your prints on fabric yourself to having them professionally manufactured?

Professional manufacturers have commercial grade equipment for digital textile printing and facilities that I do not have. Outsourcing allows me extra time to design the goods and focus on marketing, sales, and shipping. I also am guaranteed commercial grade quality, colorfastness, and consistency.

A sampling of Betsy Olmsted's work shows the brilliant colors and detail she is able to achieve through commercial grade production from the manufacturer.

How did you find the right company to trust with your work? Did you have any problems with quality of production?

This has been a long road. I started in the way described below. But now I work with someone I trust in India to produce most of my goods—we found each other through mutual business acquaintances. This company is a one-stop shop, which has been wonderful. And because we print digitally, we are able to order small quantities. They print, cut, sew, fold, tag, and package in one place. It's a dream. I have tried three different printers to get the best quality. One time I ordered 500 yards of fabric from a small printing studio in India, and the fabric was filthy and it was a disaster! I still have issues getting the color exactly right, but that's why I order samples and make adjustments before the final production run.

Photos by Elizabeth Pedinotti Haynes

Betsy had to try out several manufacturers to get the product she wanted to represent her work. Knowing you might have to try several attempts and manufacturers to get things just right should be part of your business plan.

How would you recommend (now that you have the experience!) someone start the search for a manufacturer for her own product?

Starting by looking at local resources is how I got started. Working with a local manufacturer enables you to form a relationship where you can meet in person and be hands-on with the production. The internet is a great way to find someone. Sometimes you'll need to find multiple vendors; for example, tags, labels, packaging, printing, and sewing may all come from different sources. I found that working with an established business with good customer service and written policies is the best way to protect yourself against mistakes or unsatisfactory quality.

Thank you so much, Betsy, for your honesty about searching for a manufacturing partner. It sounds like persistence and patience will pay off when you find the perfect company to work with!

Visit Betsy online:
betsyolmsted.com

SPREADING THE WORD

You may have the best, most creative, most gorgeous handmade pieces in the world to sell. You may have the most stylish and accessible website ever, but if you don't have a plan for how to get the word out about your product, all your hard work and creativity could be for nothing. Many creative business people struggle with promoting themselves and their work, but it is not as hard or mysterious as you might think. Recognizing who your customer is, making a plan to reach that customer, and setting sales goals are marketing basics that everyone can handle.

I wrote down the following quote about marketing many years ago and I love how simple and true it is:

> Marketing is used to create the customer, to keep the customer, and to satisfy the customer.

I don't know who said it, but I love how simple and true it is about your relationship with your customer. She is at the root of your business. Let's begin by talking about her. The following is aimed at online sales, but most of it can also be applied to selling in person since the root is individualizing your sales strategy.

Photo by Virginia Lindsay

This handmade doll is created for my ideal customer. She is a mom of a daughter(s) under 10. She is concerned with high quality and inspiring creative play in her child. She is willing to spend more for something really nice but is not wasteful. She is nostalgic for playtime before electronics. She lives in nice suburbs or in the city. (To make this project, see Dolly with Style, page 72.)

Identifying Your Customer

Creating an imaginary ideal customer is a great way to understand how to implement a marketing plan. If you have never done this exercise before, it is well worth your time and effort. The idea is to imagine, on paper, who your ideal customer is. Not just any customer, but the perfect person to buy what you are selling. Her exact age, her job, where she lives, who her friends are, what she looks like, how many kids she has, and so on. That might seem kind of silly until you take this person and think about how they spend their time online and shopping. If you sell organic moisture-wicking fabric headbands, who would your customer be? And then, what kinds of things would a 34-year-old, environmentally conscious, marathon running, mother of three who lives in Texas be doing on the internet?

WHERE IS SHE SPENDING HER TIME?

She would be visiting websites about green living. She would be planning healthy menus. She would be looking for organic sunscreen (it's hot and sunny in Texas). She would be visiting running mother Facebook pages or support groups. She would check out websites for running gear that would be environmentally friendly. If you are selling in person, she would be at the local 5K's, 10K's, and half-marathons getting ready for her big event. Bingo! Gearing your marketing plan toward this person will also capture potential customers on the fringe who want to be more like or have things in common with this person.

Using Social Media

You can speak directly to your specific audience in your social media outlets as well. Try to think of social media as conversation and not necessarily a sales pitch.

For example, for organic moisture-wicking fabric headbands:

- You can post about fitness that has a low impact on the environment.

- You can post about fitting your running into your schedule when you have kids.

- You can write about chemicals involved in making the standard fitness clothing and how your gear is so much better.

- You can reference healthy, organic, kid-friendly meals.

- Photograph your headbands on running women pushing jogging strollers.

- Share on Instagram your headbands in all their glorious organic colors.

- Make a video of your headbands on runners finishing a marathon.

- Post a photo of your headband on a mom serving her kids a healthy dinner and share the recipe.

- Write a blog post with your headband on a woman hiking in a national park with her family and tell about that experience.

The possibilities are endless when you feel like you are promoting to one certain type of person. You will never feel like you have nothing to say about your products if you can focus on that ideal friendly customer instead of a whole crowd of people who don't seem to be listening. Using this strategy also helps you to understand that you are not pushing anything unwanted on anyone. You are establishing trust with your customer that what you have is useful and good for their life. No tricks or lies or pushy marketing is needed when you are communicating with someone who wants what you have. But understand that social media is for socializing and making friends—not necessarily someplace people go to shop (although that seems to be changing as social media channels make it easier and easier to buy directly through their websites). Using social media is primarily so they will think of you when the time to shop does happen. It is also constantly changing and evolving so you need to have a flexible plan.

Photo by Jillian Goulding

Kendra of Swankaroo (page 39) poses kids using her backpack for Instagram posts. This helps moms to imagine their own children using the product.

Kendra from Swankaroo (page 39) says:

"In the beginning, Instagram made my business blossom! It's slowed down in its ability to connect with others since the algorithm has changed, but it's still my only social media platform. I've thought about expanding to Facebook, Snapchat, Twitter, and all other conceivable social media outlets to draw in more business, but knowing myself and how much I'm on my phone as it is, I'm resisting taking the leap and sticking to just Instagram. Networking is vital. Getting to know other shops and working together to boost your shop morale and exposure has been key to my steady growth."

Emailing Newsletters

Gathering emails for your business newsletter is promotional gold for a small business owner. This task converts more interested "social media" friends into actual paying customers than 50 Instagram posts. The social media lays a foundation of trust and interest, but an email telling about a sale, a new product, an event, or even just sewing news, really brings in the purchases. Every time you make a sale, ask if your customer will join your email list. Offer an incentive such as a discount off the next purchase or a free printable. As this email list grows, so will your online and in person sales!

MailChimp, Constant Contact, Emma, and many other online websites are created specifically to help you create great emails. They will gather your list and then give you templates to send out pretty promotions. Remember to keep it simple and email regularly (at least once every few weeks) to get the most out of your list.

Networking for Mutual Promotion

You know your ideal customer is spending time on websites that promote running, so why not make a connection with that website? Or visit that specialty store in person? Email or call and offer to send a sample. Offer to write about your area of expertise, for example, how organic sustainable fabrics are better for the environment and therefore better for runners. You might get a lot of no's or not even get a reply, but think of it as fishing and keep working until you have a nice group of contacts. The important thing to remember about these contacts is that you are in a mutually beneficial business relationship. You cannot expect them to simply promote for you without getting something in return, unless you are willing to pay for advertising.

Using Paid Advertising

Where? How much? When? How long? Paid advertising can be very beneficial if you get into the right situation.

Facebook is a great place to pay for advertising for small business because you can target exact groups of people. It is well worth $25 to spend if you make $500 on a sale you are running or a new product you are releasing. Make sure you are targeting properly though and learn the policies of Facebook because they are changing all the time!

A Facebook post such as this one is conversational but also mentions my product.

Social Media Influencers

Influential bloggers and stylists who have established credibility in a specific industry can be a great resource if you do your research and contact someone who has engagement with their audience. You can either contact these people directly by doing research yourself or there are companies like Popular Pays and MuseFind that will connect you for a fee. Think of this person as spokesperson for you—she will need to believe in your product almost as much as you do to make it worth your investment. If you can find the right person, this can be a great partnership.

Taking advantage of partnerships and online promotions can be very helpful. It is important to do your research though and make sure it is worth that chunk of your budget when there are many less expensive ways to get the word out about your business. You might be better off having a marketing professional help you!

SPOTLIGHT INTERVIEW

Lisa Jacobs of Market Your Creativity
Marketing and Establishing Relationships with Customers

To help you get inspired, here is one of my very favorite marketing gurus. Lisa Jacobs is a thought-provoking consultant on the subjects of authentic marketing, strategic business growth, and business planning. She's the author of the best-selling Your Best Year book series and writes the blog Marketing Creativity. She has helped me establish my own view of how to promote, and I know she will help you too.

Many fledgling sewing business owners start out strong but slowly start to give up when their sales either level out or start to fall. What is the first thing you would tell people to do to get back on their feet?

The first thing I explain to a fledgling business owner is the 30-90 Rule of online business, in which the work you're doing in the current 30 days won't pay off until 90 days later. Whenever you find yourself experiencing a slow period, don't blame the season. Instead, look back 90 days on your calendar to find the cause.

This information soothes creatives with a dose of information that they can quantify.

There's no such thing as instant gratification in this business.

Years ago, I taught the seven-touch rule to marketing in which you can expect to present an offer to a warm contact at least seven times before they'd buy. Additionally, I reference the twenty-step guide to advertising in which you have to advertise to a cold contact up to twenty times before they're interested. A warm contact is someone who knows and trusts you already, and a cold contact is someone who's just finding you for the first time—no trust established.

Those rules have radically changed in a short period of time. With social media, you're bombarded with sales messages in a most personal way and at every turn. Therefore, it typically takes as many as twenty touches before a warm contact buys and as many as 50 (!) introductions before a cold contact takes interest.

As you grow in business, your presence— the amount of people you attract, connect

Lisa says, "In relation to all that's happening on the internet, your business is a tiny speck in an infinite universe. As thousands, then tens of thousands, then hundreds of thousands of people find that speck, your business grows in size, reputation, and credibility."

with, and convert—grows as well. Growing larger (also known as scaling) becomes easier, because you're no longer a speck in the midst of vast and limitless space. Instead, you become a bigger presence commanding attention in the industry.

What role do you think social media plays in converting friends into customers? How big a role should it play in a marketing plan?

Social media has a huge role in making friends, but not so much in converting them. It's a superficial layer with a very conversational tone. You shouldn't ask for much on social media, and if you do ask, your expectations for receiving should be very low. I advise my clients to use social media to entice followers onto an email list and ask for the sale there.

I like how you write about establishing trust and a continuing relationship with each customer. Can you describe your ideas on this process?

There's always underlying movement between buyer and seller. It's a dance that I love, and as the business owner, you're the lead partner. Everywhere you exist online (your "sales funnel") is meant to do three things for you:

1. Attract.

2. Connect.

3. Convert.

Most people forget this when they're selling online and they get off track. Your customer wants you to keep interest in them, and it's in your best interest to keep the relationship progressing forward. Marketing, in general, is a complex process, but a simple system once you build it.

First and foremost, your customer wants to know what your product will do for them. People like to feel appreciated and served.

To start the conversation, you want to tell your customer how your product is going to make their life better, solve their problems, create happiness or more convenience, and leave them feeling satisfied with their purchase long after they check out.

Second, they want to imagine the product or service in their lives. In fact, until they envision this, *they will not buy*. They want to know how they're going to use it, where they're going to put it, and how they'll feel differently once it's over and done.

Finally, they want a powerful offer. Yes they do! They want you to take the stage and present yourself as a confident business owner who has a valuable product for sale. They're important, their time is valuable, and they want you to deliver a strong presentation.

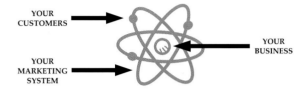

Lisa also says: "Whatever you share online lives there, like a growing orbit of attraction. The more space you claim, the more space becomes available to you. The more movement you generate around you, the more momentum you gain as a whole. Marketing is a constant presentation, and the ultimate goal is to dominate space and claim a stake in your industry. To create that growing orbit, there must be movement."

What is a common mistake you see new creative business owners making that you wish you could help them fix so their business would grow stronger?

The biggest mistake I see new creatives make is overestimating other online businesses, and underestimating themselves. I feel like a lot of my success can be attributed to my "If they can do it, I can do it" attitude.

Tony Robbins says, "Success leaves clues." That's what all the success around you is: clues. Stop letting it intimidate. Start learning from it.

Thank you so much, Lisa! I really like the concept of creating a relationship with the customer that Lisa defines so well. That is advice we can all use to grow our business!

Visit Lisa online: marketyourcreativity.com

MAKE A MARKETING PLAN

My final marketing advice is to create a calendar and marketing goals. As Lisa says, preparation is key to a successful marketing campaign. For years I would realize that Mother's Day was a week away and I could have done such a fun promotion to sell my handmade items or sewing patterns. Then I would spend a day putting together something that I thought was exciting (and it was usually pretty good!), but the timing was off and the promotion flopped.

A plan makes a huge difference. Give yourself the proper time to accomplish something before you view it as a failure. Once the plan is in place, set a sales goal. This goal can be a certain number of sales or a certain number of email addresses collected. For example, you plan a holiday promotion and set a sales goal to make $1,000. With planning and preparation, you can have your email marketing plan in place, your social media ideas, and your advertising budget already mapped out. The goal is to give you encouragement and to fuel your participation.

SEO—Search Engine Optimization

Lastly, what the heck is SEO and do you need to pay any attention to it? The answer is initially *yes* and then *not really*.

First, understand that SEO is simply the order in which someone searching on search engines (Google, Bing, Yahoo) sees your webpage and content. SEO stands for Search Engine Optimization, so it is simply the method for getting your things found when people are searching for them on the internet. The better you are at SEO, the higher on the list your business will appear. Meaning for example, if someone searches online for "organic fabric headbands for runners," you want them to see your website listed on the first page, right? Although it is a complicated algorithm that is constantly changing, some solid tactics always remain the same.

Once you set it up and learn how to use it on your website, the goal is to forget about it and let your good practices do their work. SEO is not at all intimidating but can get very complicated if you choose to get involved in the details. Simply putting the following practices into your existing strategy can help SEO work to your advantage and hopefully bring you more sales.

IMAGES

Using images to boost your SEO.

- Give your image files descriptive names. Never leave them named:
    IMG2346.tif
  Instead, name them:
    Blue-organic-running-headband.tif
  Search engines recognize hyphens as spaces and can find photos of your work when someone searches for running headbands.

- Provide ALT-tags for your images. These are readable descriptions of the image on your site for times when the image doesn't load. These descriptions should also describe the image but not repeat the filename if possible.

An example would be "Handmade Navy organic headband for fitness."

- Make sure your image files are fairly small to facilitate shorter loading time and make searching much quicker. Many online storefronts, such as Shopify and Big Cartel, will do this automatically for you, but on your own website you need to change the size of your files so they are 500 KB or less. Most editing software (such as Adobe Photoshop or Photoshop Elements) will easily change the size and keep the quality of your photos still looking great.

KEYWORDS

If the phrase "use better keywords!" doesn't have you all stressed out, you have a big advantage over me! The keyword pressure can be a bit overwhelming since all the online sales experts are constantly telling us that we will be found if we just use better keywords. But what are keywords and why are we often being told we are doing them poorly?

Here is what you need to know: Think about phrases that someone searching for your products would put into a search engine. Phrases such as "organic fabric running headband" or "handmade cloth doll with orange yarn hair" or "cross body bag with zippers in blue"—use those words in your titles and descriptions. If you are writing simple, descriptive titles, you should not have a problem with SEO keywords. The more descriptive the better so you don't compete with huge companies carrying blue headbands or cloth dolls.

It is when you get involved in naming things like "Petunia Periwinkle Bag" that you might have to get more creative. That is a great name, but it means that your item description needs to be very concise at describing your bag. Just think of keyword SEO as a computer scrolling through and picking out phrases on your website to help people find what they are searching for. Easy! No tricks are needed for you to have SEO success within your niche. Just don't get frustrated if you are trying to compete for keywords with huge companies.

Cathy Topping, founder of Your Web Toolkit (yourwebtoolkit.com) says:

"Consistent, clear, and user-friendly content is at the heart of a good SEO approach."

Cathy's website is a great resource for learning about websites and internet resources and is worth a visit for you to learn more details about SEO.

The next chapter (Streamlining Your Costs and Materials, page 37) includes an interview with Amy Richardson-Golia of June & January (page 41). She credits quite of bit of her early success to SEO and collaboration with other brands. In an interview on heymama.co, Amy says:

"I spent a lot of time reading and looking at information about how the Etsy SEO worked—using tags, organic search queries, and descriptions to get the most interested shoppers to my page. I studied what tags were working the best for Etsy sellers who had a huge number of sales and started implementing those into my own listings on Etsy. Pretty early on though, I knew the value of social media and working with bloggers to help my brand get 'found' and discovered that the more traffic I was getting from external sources, and the more sales I got from those channels, the higher my listings would show on the Etsy search page. It was all a ton of trial and error, but by the time we transitioned to our own URL we were showing at the #1 spot for 'baby headbands' on Etsy."

STREAMLINING YOUR COSTS AND MATERIALS

It's time to get serious about two very important things happening in your business that can make a huge difference in your bottom line: costs and materials. For all professional sewists, keeping track of these elements is key to boosting your business to the next level and insuring that you keep even more of the profits.

Materials

Materials need to be researched fully before you commit to making something part of your store. I personally have created a new product kit, written special instructions using specific fabrics, created special packaging, edited special photos, and invested time and money into advertising only to find out the fabric I based the whole project on went out of print almost as soon as I started. Then I had to start paying above retail for the fabric just so I could use all the effort I put into my campaign. What to be learned from this lesson? Research!

Quality is extremely important to people buying handmade. It might be smart to think about passing on that trendy print and invest in solids and basics that will still look gorgeous, be more affordable, be higher quality, and will be in stock longer. I also suggest that instead of creating a whole campaign using just one fabric, create a campaign based on a style and then introduce seasonal fabrics.

My book *Sewing to Sell* (page 127) includes information on making the best use of your fabric, including altering patterns slightly to better fit the length and width of available fabric. This can save you a lot of money and time!

Photo by Kendra Oakden

Kendra Oakden of Swankaroo (page 39) has mastered the smart tactic of keeping the same style but introducing new fabrics seasonally. This is a spring style of her classic pack.

Finding quality materials is a matter of doing research and figuring out how to get the very best possible quality for the very best price. Planning out your fabric needs in advance and doing calculations to make the best possible use of fabric is essential.

Wholesale is a great option if you plan properly. All companies have different wholesale policies and I encourage you to send emails and make calls. These products are often of higher quality than retail and much more affordable after you purchase the minimum amount.

Research wholesale companies online and then ask for samples so you know exactly what you are getting. This will be hard for those of us who like to sew when inspiration strikes, but it will be worth your efforts when you get exactly what you want. Not only can you find excellent quality fabrics online, but also wool felt, elastic, hook-and-loop tape, pillow forms, webbing, specialty buttons, and more!

If you are going to go this route, understand that you will need that make that initial large investment and if you are a solo shop doing all your own sewing, you need to be pretty confident that you will use up all that fabric. Basics, such as the Tinted Denim from Cloud9 Fabrics that I used in my Foxy-Boxy Travel Duffle (page 117), could be a smart choice, but prints that might go out of style might *not* be the best choice.

Buying fabric by the bolt is the most cost-effective way to purchase fabric.

Working Smart

Being a good worker when you are your own boss is sometimes a real challenge. It's easy to get distracted and not make good use of your time. Your time is money. Be prepared for your workday by making comprehensive lists, accomplishing daily goals and chipping away at long-term goals. Reserve time not just for sewing but also making important business decisions and promotions. One place that I get really bogged down in is making decisions regarding materials. I need to get a new

seasonal product going and I simply go 'round and 'round wasting time trying to decide. Last year I finally decided to set a timer and just get the job done. This helped me to avoid wasted time and got me to use my work schedule more efficiently.

Here to share their business secrets are two successful ladies who have taken different paths with their businesses but are still running things happily their own way.

Kendra Oakden of Swankaroo
Business Secrets

Kendra Oakden, creator and founder of Swankaroo, has been making adorable backpacks and mini purses since 2013. Kendra's backpacks have been featured in many magazines and online design blogs. She has more than 30,000 Instagram followers and regularly sells out of her products.

You have created a simple yet adorable and useful product line with your backpacks and mini purses for Swankaroo. Did you begin by sewing these things yourself in your home? Where are they made now?

Swankaroo began in my parents' garage, then eighteen months into my business, I outsourced my pattern and design to a local warehouse. They were in charge of production from the beginning to the end. While it was great to be able to free up some time, I found that for me personally this created more stress as my turnaround times actually became longer, depending on my place in the queue in the warehouse's production line.

Communication and language barriers made it frustrating at times for changes to be made, and after a year I decided to take everything back into my own hands. I was worried about how I would handle the production again all on my own, but so far the work has been worth the control I gained back over my business. I've been so much happier knowing everything is back in my hands.

The materials on your backpacks are simple and stylish. How do you find your materials? Not just the cotton fabric, but the faux leather and other hardware?

My materials come from a variety of sources. I've scoured the web trying to find the best quality and price for all my supplies. But most of it comes from big sites, such as Fabric.com, Spoonflower, and eBay.

The simple design of your pieces leads me to believe you are making smart use of your materials with very little waste. Can you talk a little bit about that process and how you have worked on it over the years?

Actually, my design really stems from my lack of sewing ability. I don't have patience or skill to come up with an intricate pattern, so this design is something simple I can work with that makes for quick cutting, and yes, little waste because of the basic lines. I haven't varied much from my pattern over the years, so the process has stayed the same. My husband is the only other member of our production team, so together he and I have come up with a system of who cuts what to maximize the use of our time, space, and efficiency.

Wasting little fabric allows Swankaroo to invest in high-quality fabrics to really make their product look great.

What are your goals for the future of Swankaroo?

My goal is to just keep the shop steady. I love where I am with the shop right now. I am so fortunate to have this creative outlet. I like feeling industrious and I am super-flattered that my handiwork is out there in the world. But I don't want to expand. I've got four little kids at home, and every day it becomes more apparent to me that they are growing at a rapid rate, and I want to savor their childhood. I feel so blessed to be able to contribute to our family's income, stay at home with the kids, and be a part of a wonderful handmade community.

Thank you so much, Kendra! It is amazing to see all that you have created on your own. It appears that hard work and focus have really paid off for Swankaroo!

Visit Kendra online: swankaroo.storenvy.com

Amy Richardson-Golia of June & January
Business Savvy

Amy Richardson-Golia is the CEO of the kid's clothing company June and January. Her vision and business savvy have propelled a handmade business that started at her kitchen table to a hugely successful business with celebrity endorsements. June & January focuses on classic basics in bright beautiful colors, high-quality fabrics, and affordable prices.

I know you started June & January at your kitchen table and now it is a successful small business with nine employees and goods sold around the world. What made you take the leap from the sewing machine on your table to selling on such a big scale?

After about a year and a half of sewing everything myself (or with the help of other sewists) I realized that there were so many styles I wanted to introduce but simply wouldn't be able to construct them on my own given my machinery and space limitations—so I began looking into manufacturing in early 2013. It was a long and daunting process, but once I had committed to that, I really had no choice but to make it work and go bigger scale.

What brought you to focus on the primary colors and simple designs that are the cornerstone of your brand? Many hobby sewers get caught up in trying to do too much and selling too many different things when they begin their business. How did you avoid this common pitfall?

I definitely was guilty of the "too much" mentality—the first manufacturer we had in 2013 saw that I was struggling with the idea of so many styles, so many prints, and so many combinations, and he gave me some of the best advice—go narrow and deep. It was some of the best words of wisdom I've ever received to date. I lived by that mentality from that point on and started to introduce more basic, solid colors into the lineup, and they were so successful. We still follow the narrow and deep ideology, but we're able to do it on a larger scale as our production allows.

A bin full of pink bows ready for packaging and shipment to June & January customers

What was your original marketing strategy to grow your business at the beginning? How has that strategy evolved?

Very early on I was using social media as a platform to share our products. I also saw the benefit of working with other people (bloggers, especially) who had their own large audience and began partnering with them to bring awareness to our brand. We still work very closely with bloggers, influencers, and release partners and continue to lean on social media as our number one traffic source—we just do so with a larger budget!

Your online store is bright, simple, and gorgeous. What advice would you give to people to make their online presence more professional and effective?

Truly know your audience. Our customers are busy moms who don't want to spend hours browsing a website trying to find their favorite pieces, so we made it clean and quick and created an intuitive shopping experience. In my experience, when it comes to a website, less is more.

Bright, colorful fabrics are a signature of June & January.

How do you develop new concepts? Are you still doing the sewing or are you just the business side now? What inspired you to keep growing June & January?

When we transitioned to manufacturing in 2013, I made a choice to take a break from sewing (both for business and pleasure), and I haven't touched a machine since. Taking a hobby and making it a profitable company really ruined the experience for me, and I've had no interest in really being creative in that way (plus I just don't have the time anymore).

I work closely with a production director on developing all new products. We usually start from sketches or from me just shooting random ideas at her, and then the sketches are sent to our sample room in China where they're sewn up and sent back to us for revisions and eventually approval. A lot of the growth of the company has come by surprise, the past few years have been a major snowball effect, and now that we have a team, all but one are mothers themselves. I am really motivated to provide and cultivate a work-team culture that everyone loves to be part of and is proud to be behind.

Thank you so much, Amy! Your work to expand your business is impressive and inspires us all to work hard and take risks!

Visit Amy online: juneandjanuary.com

SMALL BUSINESS FINANCE

When it comes to small business finance, this is a great time to be a sole proprietor or a small business. There are so many tools available to make the tedious tasks of counting your pennies less time-consuming and more accurate than ever.

Accounting

As a small business owner, the most important thing is to create income and expense categories so you can accurately keep track of what you spend and what you earn.

If you are not ready to set up a business bank account, get a PayPal debit card that is connected with your PayPal account and use it for all your business expenses. Many people use PayPal to purchase handmade goods, and you should be able to have enough money in your account to pay for most of your materials and online fees. For larger expenses, you can still use the debit card but have it connected to a bank account that can cover any larger expenses. This way, you can still keep track of that expense and be able to find it for your taxes at the end of the year, even if that large expense is pulled from your main personal account.

Come tax time, you can create a spreadsheet (using Microsoft Excel or Apple Numbers) that categorizes all these expenses. If your business is still pretty small, this might be a bit tedious but shouldn't be too bad if you have all your expenses on the PayPal debit card. This is how I ran my business for several years and it worked just fine. As most online shops accept multiple forms of payment, you will also need to add the income from those other payment forms onto your spreadsheet.

Being consistent and setting up a simple system from January 1 to December 31 is the key. Then, hand this information about your income and expenses to a tax professional or carefully fill out those tax forms yourself. You can purchase specific spreadsheets for creative sellers such as those made by Janet LeBlanc of Paper + Spark (paperandspark.com). These will guide you to not only be prepared for tax season, they will also help you with pricing and inventory.

When using spreadsheets gets too be too much, an excellent way to make things easier on yourself is to start integrating with online accounting software, such as QuickBooks (by Intuit, quickbooks.intuit.com). This online system tracks all your income and expenses for you by integrating with your business bank account. You'll spend some time setting up categories but after that initial time investment, QuickBooks takes care of the bookkeeping for you.

For example, if you purchase some organic cotton spandex (back to those headbands) using your business account, QuickBooks will automatically put that expense into your materials category. If you have lunch with a store owner who wants to stock your headband, and you use your business card, QuickBooks will put that in the entertainment category of your expenses. You must log in once every few weeks and approve of these expenses.

It also tracks all your income in one place and will let you know where you are making the most money and where your efforts are not working as well. You can regularly check in and see what is working and then make adjustments. Perhaps all those Etsy fees are not as well spent as you thought, when you can view the cost versus income. You can make adjustments as needed throughout your work year. QuickBooks can even help you pay employees and can do all the withholding taxes for you. This system does cost about $35 to $75 a month, but many small business owners find themselves saving so much time that the expense is well worth it. In addition to this, QuickBooks can integrate directly with PayPal, your credit cards, and multiple bank accounts.

Inventory

Is it really worth the time and effort?

Yes and *yes.*

USING INVENTORY TRACKING TO STAY ORGANIZED

Keeping careful inventory of not only what you have made but also your supplies gives you the best overview of how your business is going. Knowing just how much you have of everything will also keep you from having to drop everything and run to the store and pay *retail* for things you could easily have gotten wholesale if you had been more organized. Being organized doesn't necessarily come naturally to many creative people who just want to make beautiful things, but there are many helpful resources and easy habits to implement into your work life that can make things easier.

USING INVENTORY TRACKING TO CALCULATE YOUR PRICES

Keeping close track of your supplies, how much you ordered and how much they cost will help you with pricing. A good pricing formula is:

Supplies + Labor + Overhead = Wholesale

Wholesale × 2 = Your retail price

- **Supplies:** The cost of supplies is pretty easy to work out when you keep track of how much you spent on your supplies and how much you use to make each item.

- **Labor:** How much you want to make per hour is up to you.

- **Overhead:** This is the sum of all those extra expenses you pay to Etsy, PayPal, Facebook, advertising, rent, and so on. Overhead is harder to track, but after you have been in business awhile, you can look back over a year of those expenses, total it all together, and divide it by the number of items you are selling.

Knowing how much you spent can ensure that you are charging enough for your items.

USING INVENTORY TRACKING FOR TAXES

Tracking expenses for tax purposes is a little tricky because you can only claim the expenses that you spent on things that you actually sold. For example, when you purchase bolts of fabric, you can only claim on your taxes the cost of the fabric that you made into things and actually sold. In other words, if you used half the fabric to make 100 items for a show, and you sold 70 items, you are able to claim expenses only on the materials used for those 70 pieces—not the material still left on your shelf and not the 30 pieces left unsold. The good news is that you get to continue using that material and claiming it as an expense as you sell those remaining 30 pieces.

Because you can only claim tax deductions for materials and other expenses related to actual sales, keeping track of your supplies and an inventory of completed items is as essential as keeping track of your sales.

For things such as thread that are hard to quantify per item, keep track of how much you use per year and write it off as an expense that way.

> For example:
>
> You bought $360 worth of fabric in March 2017 and used half ($180 worth) to make 100 backpacks in 2017. That means you spent $1.80 per backpack.
>
> In 2017, you sold 70 of the backpacks made from that fabric. Your tax-deductible expense for those items in 2017 is $1.80 × 70 = $126.
>
> In 2018, you sell the remaining 30 of those backpacks, so you can claim $54 as a tax-deductible expense.

INVENTORY SYSTEMS

Using spreadsheets is one way to track inventory. Kelly McCants of Modern June (page 16) ran a pretty big operation with her traveling craft shows, using a spreadsheet system that helped her stay organized and led to bigger success. Kelly says:

"I used [Apple] Numbers documents to keep track of my inventory. Each show had a separate file, and I kept track of previous shows within it. I recorded what we took and what we sold—doing so prevented me from relying on my memory to prep for the next show. These files were a turning point, and using this system helped me immensely."

Products are available to help you keep track of your inventory. Janet LeBlanc of Paper + Spark (page 43) has also created inventory spreadsheets specifically for people selling on Etsy and her website is a fantastic resource for information on how to handle your accounting and inventory to get ready for tax seasons. Software companies, such as Stitch Labs, will take your inventory details and do all the work for you.

Whatever inventory path you choose to take, remember that it can help you run your business run more efficiently and take a lot of the guessing out of pricing and tax time.

Taxes

The main reason you're keeping these accurate records is so that you can accurately file your taxes. Then the easiest thing to do is to categorize the business expense into the same categories that are used on the Federal Tax Return, IRS Schedule C, such as:

- Advertising
- Car or truck expenses
- Insurance
- Office expense
- Travel expenses
- Supplies
- Cost of goods sold
- Equipment rental

These are all common business expenses that you'll want to track so that you can present an accurate picture of your business on your taxes.

Many of us happily work from our home and a benefit to this is that you can report the expenses for the business use of your home.

Depending on how much of your home you use, it's possible that some improvements to your home, utilities, and other regular home expenses may be deductible as well.

After you have your income and expenses tracked, you can use software such as TurboTax (by Intuit, turbotax.intuit.com) small business to file your taxes. This is very comprehensive software and covers all the bases, but take your time and make sure to answer the questions accurately. After you do it a few times, you will know most of the papers and forms that you need, but the first time through, there will probably a lot of stop and go.

TurboTax can also be integrated with QuickBooks (see Accounting, page 43) and can make filing your taxes very simple if you upgrade to a small business (paid) version of TurboTax. This costs about $100 instead of the free version. Again, you have to decide for yourself if it is worth it! But the integration of these two makes for a fast and accurate tax season and we all love that!

Hiring Financial Professionals

Depending on your business and your personal skills and interests, you might find it well worth the expense to hire some professionals and spend your time focusing on sewing and creating. But you still need to keep good records so you can go to the professionals prepared come tax season. If you've tracked your expenses and income it is going to make your office visit that much less of an effort.

Betsy Olmsted (page 26) says hiring a professional bookkeeper and tax professional was one of the best business moves she ever made:

"I use an independent bookkeeper who logs into all my payment and income services. We also take inventory and give her that information so she can factor it in. She keeps track of everything and prepares it for the accountant for taxes. Keeping track of my finances properly is not my strength and takes a lot of time. The bookkeeper is a huge stress relief. The reports she produces are really helpful for assessing where there is need to cut back on expenses and where I need to increase sales or make pricing changes in order to make the business financially successful. It helps to see which products sell best and worst and keep some in production while retiring others. She also separates my income from licensing versus retail versus wholesale so I can compare and figure out where to drive the business next."

Amy Frank (page 11), creator of Mindfully Made Studios and owner of The Makery in State College, Pennsylvania, says:

"Accounting is my kryptonite—seriously! The best thing I did, and I only did it recently, is to hire an accountant to truly outsource my bookkeeping and accounting."

PROJECTS

Handmade takes time. In order to make the best use of your time, it's important to choose and make products that are beautiful and show your individual talents, but are not going to bog you down in details and time consuming techniques. The following projects fit this description— perhaps not the first time you sew them. But as you become familiar with the project and add your own stamp to the design, you will be able to complete these fairly quickly and they will look great.

IMPORTANT NOTE

You have permission to make and sell the projects in this book!

This is not the case for all projects/patterns that you find online or in books and magazines—*be sure to read the copyright before you plan to make and sell items using designs or patterns that you did not create yourself.* Some will allow you to make and sell the items (or a limited number of items), but many will not—please respect all copyright restrictions.

LITTLE TIME,
Big Results

CIRCLE AROUND PILLOWS

SUGGESTED PRICE POINT
$28 TO $38

Finished size: 12″ × 12″

Pillows with personality are like handmade gold. The trick to making and selling them? They are original and cute but fairly quick to make. You can get really bogged down in detail when it comes to making handmade pillows but this circle shape is easy to customize into a lot of different characters. For these three, I've added the petals, sun's rays, and lion mane, but feel free to experiment with other ideas and give them your own handmade character.

Supplies and Cutting

Makes 1 pillow.

COTTON FABRIC

- 1 square 10″ × 10″ for front
- 1 square 12″ × 12″ for back

WOOL FELT

Flower:

- **Assorted pinks:** 4 pieces 3″ × 20″ for petals and cheeks

Lion:

- **White:** 1 piece 2″ × 4″ for muzzle
- **Pink:** 1 piece 3″ × 4½″ for nose
- **Black:** 1 piece 1″ × 4″ for eyes and nose tip
- **Brown:** 1 piece 6″ × 29½″ for mane

Sun:

- **Black:** 1 piece 1″ × 2″ for eyes
- **Orange:** 1 piece 1″ × 6″ for eyelids

OTHER SUPPLIES

- **Midweight fusible interfacing:** 1 piece 10″ × 10″ (such as Pellon 931TD)
- **Embroidery floss and needle**
- **Polyester fiberfill**

Optional:

- **Piping or other trim:** 1 yard for each pillow

Construction

Seam allowances are ¼″ unless otherwise noted.

FOR ALL PILLOWS

1. Fuse the interfacing to the wrong side of the 10″ × 10″ fabric.

2. From the Circle Around Pillows patterns (pullout page P2), trace a 10″ circle and a 12″ circle onto the 10″ and 12″ squares of fabric.

For the facial features, follow the specific instructions your desired pillow.

FABRICS USED: Wool felt from National Nonwovens and cotton from my stash

MAKE THE FLOWER PILLOW

1. Trace the eyes, nose, and lips from the flower pillow pattern onto the 10″ fabric circle. Cut out the cheeks from wool felt. Use the petal pattern to cut about 24 flower petals from the felt.

2. Using the photo as a guide, sew the cheek pieces onto the 10″ circle. Embroider the face onto the flower pillow using your choice of stitches. Now cut out both circles.

3. Sew piping to the perimeter of the 10″ circle, if desired.

4. Pinch the center of the petals to give them some dimension and pin them onto the 10″ circle with the rounded end facing in toward the center. Continue pinching the centers and pinning the petals until you have done about 12 petals and you are about halfway around the circle. The petals should overlap slightly. Then sew the petals in place and remove the pins. Continue pinching and pinning petals the rest of the way around the 10″ circle. Sew the rest of the petals in place.

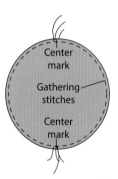

Attach the petals to the 10″ circle.

5. Fold the 12″ circle into quarters and make 4 evenly spaced marks with a water- or air-soluble pen: top and bottom and left and right.

6. Set your sewing machine to the longest stitch. Begin sewing without a backstitch ½″ from the top mark and all the way around to ½″ from the bottom mark. Do not backstitch. Pull thread out about 6″ and cut. Then, start again ½″ from the bottom and come around to the top. Again, no backstitch and leave 6″ threads. This will create a gathering stitch.

Sew gathering stitches on each side of the 12″ circle.

7. On the wrong side of the 10″ circle, mark the top, bottom, left, and right with a water- or air-soluble pen.

8. With right sides facing, pin the top mark of the 10″ piece to the top mark of the 12″ piece. Then pin the bottom marks together, the

right marks together, and then the left marks together. Make sure the pins are not at the very edge.

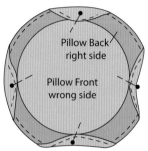

Pin the circles together, matching the marks.

9. Gently pull on the threads to gather half of the 12″ circle until it matches the side of the 10″ circle. Adjust the gathering until it looks even. Then repeat for the other side of the 12″ circle.

10. Add extra pins to hold the pieces in place and sew together the 2 sides. Leave a 4½″ gap to turn it right side out.

11. Turn the pillow right side out and stuff it with polyester fiberfill.

12. Hand sew the opening closed.

MAKE THE LION PILLOW

1. Trace the mouth and whiskers from the lion pillow pattern onto the 10″ fabric circle. Cut out the nose, muzzle, and eyes from wool felt.

2. Using the photo as a guide, sew the face pieces onto the 10″ circle. Embroider the rest of the lion face, using your choice of stitches. Now cut out both circles.

3. Add piping around the 10″ circle, if you wish.

4. Sew together the 6″ edges of the 6″ × 29½″ piece of brown felt to make a loop.

Fold the piece wrong sides together so that the seam is on the inside. You'll now have a loop 3″ wide. Use long machine stitches to baste about ⅛″ from the raw edges.

5. Make 2½″ cuts spaced every 1″ to make loops for the lion's mane. Start your cuts at the folded edge and be careful not to cut through your basting stitches.

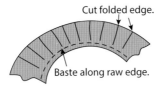
Cut folded edge.
Baste along raw edge.

6. Sew the felt onto the 10″ circle with the folded edge of the loops facing in toward the center.

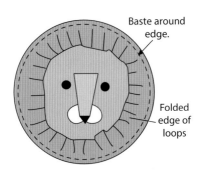
Baste around edge.
Folded edge of loops

7. Follow the instructions for Make the Flower Pillow, Steps 5–12 (previous page).

MAKE THE SUN PILLOW

1. Trace the nose, mouth, and lower eyelines from the sun pillow pattern onto the 10″ fabric circle. Cut out the eyes and eyelids from wool felt.

2. Using the photo as a guide, sew the face pieces onto the 10″ circle. Embroider the rest of the sun face, using your choice of stitches. Now cut out both circles.

3. Add piping or other trim around the perimeter of the circle, if desired.

4. Cut 15 of the 3″ triangle pattern from yellow felt and 11 of the 2″ triangle pattern from orange felt.

5. Arrange the yellow triangles evenly around the 10″ circle and sew them in place.

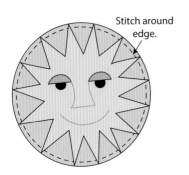
Stitch around edge.

6. Arrange the orange triangles on top of the yellow and sew them in place.

7. Follow the instructions for Make the Flower Pillow, Steps 5–12 (previous page).

Make It Your Own

- A monster would also be really cute with fur trim and felt ears. Use bright bold colors and add fun teeth.

- Make fabric petals for the flower using a variety of cute scrap fabrics.

- Use patchwork for the 12″ circle to add interest to the back of the pillow.

- Be sure to play around with fun colors and facial expressions!

ZIP AROUND ORGANIZER

SUGGESTED
PRICE POINT
$22 TO $32

Finished size: *6″ × 9″ closed*

This fun little organizer is sure to please your customers. Promote it for travel, coupons, and extra storage for a purse. You can easily make this from canvas and promote it to men as well. I worked to make the zipper as easy to install as possible—the key is to clip around the zipper corners and reduce bulk by not fusing the interfacing all the way to the corners. Once you make the first one, your creativity will be bursting to add your own unique style to this clever design.

Supplies

Makes 1 organizer.

COTTON FABRIC

- **Fabric 1 (pineapples):**
  ⅓ yard
  (*Note:* If you are using a directional print, you might need ½ yard, depending on the print.)

- **Fabric 2 (yellow):**
  1 fat quarter

- **Fabric 3 (green):**
  1 fat quarter or large scraps

OTHER SUPPLIES

- **Fusible fleece:** 1 piece 9½″ × 13½″ (one-sided, such as Fusible Warm Fleece 1 by The Warm Company)

- **Midweight fusible interfacing:** 20″ wide, ½ yard (such as Pellon 931TD)

- **Nylon zipper:** 24″ long

- **Zipper foot:** For your sewing machine

Cutting

For making multiples of 4 organizers, refer to the fabric cutting guides (below right).

FABRIC 1 (PINEAPPLES)

- 1 piece 9½″ × 13½″ for exterior

- 1 piece 7″ × 12″ for paper pocket

- 1 piece 9½″ × 9½″ for lining pocket

FABRIC 2 (YELLOW)

- 1 piece 9½″ × 13½″ for lining

FABRIC 3 (GREEN)

- 1 piece 4″ × 10″ for pen pocket

- 1 piece 2″ × 3″ for finishing the zipper

MIDWEIGHT FUSIBLE INTERFACING

- 1 piece 9″ × 13″ for lining

- 1 piece 4″ × 4¾″ for pen pocket

- 1 piece 9″ × 4½″ for lining pocket

- 1 piece 6½″ × 5¾″ for paper pocket

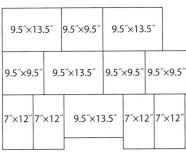

Fabric 1: 31″ × 42″

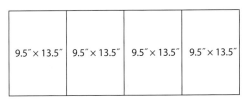

Fabric 2: 38″ × 13½″

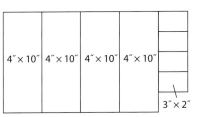

Fabric 3: 19″ × 10″

- -

Fabric cutting guides to make 4 organizers

- -

FABRICS USED: Pineapples Lemon from the Jetsetter collection from Dear Stella; Tinted Denim in Yellow from Cloud9 Fabrics; and Essex Linen Blend in Seafoam from Robert Kaufman Fabrics

Construction

Seam allowances are ¼˝ unless otherwise noted.

SEW THE ZIPPER TO THE EXTERIOR

1. Fuse the fusible fleece to the wrong side of the exterior piece.

2. Mark the top and bottom center of the 13½˝ sides with pins.

3. Open the zipper up all the way. Be careful not to twist the zipper tapes during this process.

4. Fold the separated ends of the zipper over to the wrong side to create a 45° angle, keeping the zipper stops exposed. Hold them in place with your fingers and then pin the right side of the zipper to the right side of the exterior piece on either side of the marked center of the bottom edge of the fabric. The zipper teeth should be facing in toward the center of the fabric.

5. Pin one side of the zipper out toward the bottom corner of the fabric. When you get to the corner, make 3–4 snips on the zipper tape so that it will curve easily around the corner. The snips should be less than ¼˝. The zipper will make a natural curve at the corner instead of the sharp 90° angle. Continue pinning both sides of the zipper all the way around the perimeter of the exterior and snipping at the corners.

Pin the open zipper around the edges, right side facing the fabric. Clip the zipper edges at the corners.

6. Continue pinning on either side until you get to the top center. You will see that the zipper is about 4˝ longer than needed. Stop pinning about ½˝ on either side of the center mark.

7. Using a zipper foot on your machine, sew the zipper around the exterior perimeter. At the top, gradually curve the zipper toward the center of the fabric and stop stitching ½˝ on either side of the centerline. This will allow the edge to bend easily when you sew the exterior and lining together later. The zipper tape will loop under itself at the top.

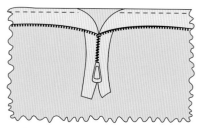

Angle the top of the zipper.

8. Clip off the fabric corners to match the zipper curve.

MAKE THE RIGHT SIDE LINING POCKETS

1. Center and fuse the interfacing to the lining piece.

2. Press the pen pocket in half, wrong sides together, so that the piece is 4˝ × 5˝. Open the piece back up and fuse interfacing to one half, using the fold line as a guide. Fold wrong sides together and sew up both the 5˝ sides. Clip the corners at the folded top and turn the piece right side out. Press and then topstitch across the folded edge.

3. Press the lining pocket piece in half, wrong sides together, so that it measures 9½˝ × 4¾˝. Open the piece back up and fuse interfacing to one half using the center fold line as a guide. Fold back together. Then, topstitch across the folded edge.

4. Press the paper pocket in half, right sides together, so that it measures 7˝ × 6˝. Open the piece back up and fuse the interfacing to one half using the fold line as a guide. Fold back right sides together. Sew up one 6˝ side that's adjacent to the folded edge. Clip the corner and turn right side out. Press and then topstitch across the top folded edge.

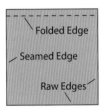

Sew up just one 6˝ side of the paper pocket.

5. Center the pen pocket on top of the paper pocket with the raw edges on the bottom matching. Sew up the sides of the pen pocket. Then sew 2 vertical lines evenly spaced (about 1˝ apart) to make 3 pocket spaces for pens.

Add the pen pocket to paper pocket.

ADD THE POCKET TO THE LINING

1. Mark the center of the lining bottom. Pin the paper pocket to the right of the mark. Match the 2 raw edges of the paper pocket to the right and bottom edges of the lining and baste them in place. Sew up the left side of the pocket to attach the pocket to the lining.

2. Place the lining pocket on the left 9½˝ edge. Line up the raw edges and baste in place. Mark the center of the 9½˝ edge and sew a divider across the pocket toward the center of the lining piece.

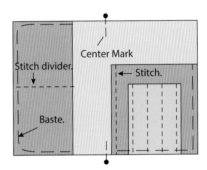

Arrange the pockets on the lining.

SEW THE EXTERIOR AND LINING TOGETHER

1. Use your iron to press the zipper corners flat toward the center. Don't overpress and melt the zipper, but press so that it lies nice and flat.

2. Place the lining and exterior right sides together. Place pins or clips at the corners and a few on the sides.

3. Use the stitches from sewing on the zipper on the wrong side of the exterior as a guide and sew the exterior and lining together.

Make sure that the end of the zipper is tucked inside between the 2 pieces. Leave a 4″ opening on the bottom edge of the lining for turning.

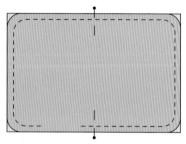

Sew the exterior and lining together, leaving a 4″ opening for turning.

4. Clip the corners and trim the bulky seams. Turn the piece right side out. Poke out the corners carefully and press flat.

5. Hand stitch the opening closed with a blind hem stitch.

6. Mark the center again and draw a line with chalk or water- or air-soluble marker. Topstitch down the center to make the divider fold easily.

FINISH THE END OF THE ZIPPER

1. With the organizer opened in front of you, zip the zipper closed until it meets the fabric—there should be about 3½″ of extra zipper. Clip off 2″ from the end so you have about 1½″ of extra zipper tape.

2. Using the 2″ × 3″ piece of fabric, press both 2″ ends toward the center ¼″, wrong sides together. Press the 2½″ raw edges in toward the center, wrong sides together, to meet in the middle. Then, press the piece in half so that it measures 1″ × 1¼″.

3. Slip the zipper end inside, pin, and sew in place ⅛″ from the edges.

Make It Your Own

- Change up the pocket configuration to suit your needs but pay attention to keeping the bulk away from the corners so the zipper can close easily.

- Experiment with fabrics, such as canvas, linen, and even leather accents, to make this piece even more special.

- Omit the zipper entirely for a much quicker project.

- The sizing can be adjusted for a much bigger piece or smaller piece. This size is designed to fit a 5″ × 8″ paper pad. So when you change your sizing, start with the paper pad size since the pockets can be variable.

CROSS YOUR HEART BAG

SUGGESTED
PRICE POINT
$20 TO $32

Finished size: 8″ × 10″

These cross body bags can be made with many options and fun fabrics. You can change things to make this bag better for your customers, but I would not change the adjustable strap option. With an adjustable strap, one bag can work for people of many sizes. Adults and kids love to have a small fun bag to carry essentials. You can market to travelers, parents, and even tweens!

Supplies

Makes 1 bag.

COTTON FABRIC

- **Fabric 1 (stripe):** 1 fat quarter
- **Fabric 2 (yellow):** 1 fat quarter
- **Fabric 3 (print):** 1 fat quarter
- **Fabric 4 (lining):** 1 fat quarter

OTHER SUPPLIES

- **Midweight fusible interfacing:** 20″ wide, ½ yard (such as Pellon 931TD)
- **Midweight cotton webbing:** 1″ wide, 1 piece 6″ long and 1 piece 55″ long
- **Hook-and-loop tape:** 1″ wide, 1 piece 6″ long
- **Button:** ¾″ diameter
- **Rectangle rings:** 1″ size, 2 rings
- **Tri-glide slide:** 1″ size, 1 slide
- **Nylon or metal zipper:** 8″ long
- **Zipper and buttonhole feet:** For your sewing machine

Cutting

For making multiples of 3 bags, refer to the fabric cutting guides (next page).

FABRIC 1 (STRIPE)

- 2 pieces 9″ × 11″ for lining
- 1 piece 9″ × 4″ for exterior front top

FABRIC 2 (YELLOW)

- 1 piece 9″ × 7½″ for exterior front bottom
- 1 piece 9″ × 11″ for exterior back

FABRIC 3 (PRINT)

- 1 piece 9″ × 15″ for exterior back pocket
- 1 piece 6″ × 12″ for lining pocket
- 2 pieces 1″ × 4″ for zipper pocket ends
- 2 pieces 4″ × 7″ for flap

FABRIC 4 (LINING)

- 2 pieces 9″ × 7″ for exterior front pocket lining

MIDWEIGHT FUSIBLE INTERFACING

- 1 piece 9″ × 7½″ for exterior front bottom
- 1 piece 9″ × 4″ for exterior front top
- 1 piece 9″ × 11″ for exterior back
- 1 piece 9″ × 7½″ for exterior back pocket
- 1 piece 6″ × 6″ for lining pocket

FABRICS USED: Chambray Rules in Cream with Black Stripe by Kathy Hall for Andover Fabrics; Chambray in Mustard from Andover Fabrics; Solar System Navy from Supernova collection by Rae Ritchie for Dear Stella; and Tinted Denim from Cloud9 Fabrics

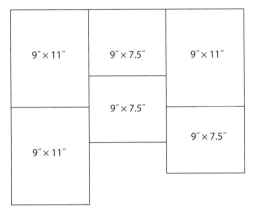

Fabric 1: 22˝ × 36˝

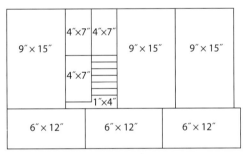

Fabric 2: 18˝ × 27˝

Fabric 3: 15˝ × 36˝

**Fabric cutting guides to make 3 bags
(excluding front pocket lining)**

Construction

Seam allowances are ¼˝ unless otherwise noted.

MAKE THE EXTERIOR PIECES

1. Press the 9˝ × 15˝ exterior pocket piece in half, wrong sides together, to make a piece 9˝ × 7½˝. Open back up and fuse the 9˝ × 7½˝ interfacing in place on half of the wrong side of fabric, using the fold as a guide. The interfaced side will be the outside of the pocket.

2. On the other half, measure ½˝ from the fold, and pin half of the hook-and-loop tape centered in place on the right side of the fabric. Sew around the perimeter of the tape.

3. Fold the piece back in place with wrong sides together. Topstitch ¼˝ from the fold and place this piece to the side for now.

4. Fuse interfacing to the wrong side of the other 3 exterior pieces: front bottom, back, and front top.

5. Measure 4˝ down from the top of the exterior back piece and mark with a pin. Center the other half of the hook-and-loop tape below the pin and pin in place. Take the exterior back pocket that you set aside earlier and press the hook-and-loop tape pieces together. Make sure that the pocket edges match up with the exterior back edges and adjust the position of the hook-and-loop tape if necessary. Then remove the pocket and sew the tape in place around its perimeter. Put the pocket back in place and baste it to the back exterior piece ⅛˝ from the edge around the perimeter of the pieces.

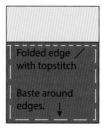

The hook-and-loop tape will hold the pocket to the back piece, but baste to make sure it lies flat.

6. Loop the 6˝ piece of 1˝ strap through the 2 rectangle 1˝ rings and move the rings to the center of the strap. Fold together the strap and use the zipper foot to sew close to the loop and secure it in place.

7. Baste the 55˝ strap to the exterior back ¾˝ from the edge on the top. Baste the folded strap (from Step 6) ¾˝ from the other side.

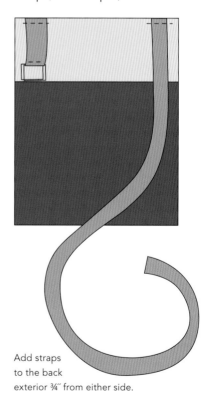

Add straps to the back exterior ¾˝ from either side.

MAKE THE FLAP

1. Fuse interfacing to the wrong side of both 4˝ × 7˝ flap pieces.

2. Sew the pieces, right sides together, down a long 7˝ edge, across the bottom 4˝ edge, and up the other 7˝ edge.

3. Clip the corners and turn right side out. Press.

4. Center the flap on the top back exterior piece and baste.

ADD THE ZIPPER TO THE EXTERIOR

1. Press the ends of the 1˝ × 4˝ pieces ¼˝ toward the wrong side so the pieces measure 1˝ × 3½˝. Press them in half, wrong sides together. The pieces should now measure 1˝ × 1¾˝.

2. Open the 8˝ zipper a few inches. Trim off both ends of the zipper to remove the stopper hardware, but be sure to *not* trim off the zipper pull.

3. Sandwich the folded fabrics from Step 1 over the zipper ends. Keep the zipper open a few inches. Pin the ends in place so that the length of the zipper and the ends is now 9˝.

4. Topstitch the folded zipper ends in place. By adding fabric to the zipper ends, you reduce bulk, and the front of the bag lies nice and flat.

Add end tabs to the zipper.

5. Use a zipper foot to sew the 9″ × 4″ exterior front piece and one side of the zipper right sides together. Then sew the other side of the zipper right sides together with the 9″ × 7½″ piece. Press flat.

6. Pin one of the right sides of the 9″ × 7″ pocket lining pieces to the wrong side of the zipper. Use the stitches from sewing the exterior to the zipper as your guide to sew this piece to the wrong side of the zipper. Then do the same with the other side of the zipper and the other 9″ × 7″ pocket lining piece.

7. Press both the lining pieces down toward the base of the exterior bottom piece. Switch back to your regular presser foot. Sew the bottom 9″ edges of the pocket lining together. The pocket pieces should be a little shorter than the exterior piece.

8. Baste the side edges of the pocket to the front exterior ⅛″ from the edge.

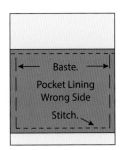

After attaching the front pocket lining pieces to the zipper, sew just the bottom of the 2 sides together.

9. Sew the front and back exterior pieces right sides together down the 2 sides and across the base.

10. Pinch the base corners together and sew a 1″ gusset on both sides.

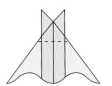

Pinch the corners together to make a 1″ gusset at the corners of the exterior.

MAKE THE LINING POCKET

1. Press the 6″ × 12″ piece of fabric in half, right sides together, to make a 6″ × 6″ piece. Open the piece back up and fuse interfacing to one half of the piece.

2. Fold the piece right sides together and pin. Sew down the sides and across the bottom, leaving a 3″ opening for turning.

3. Clip the corners and turn the piece right side out. Gently poke out the corners and press flat. Press the opening under to match the seam.

4. Topstitch across the folded edge of the pocket piece.

5. Center the pocket onto one of the 9″ × 11″ lining pieces. Pin in place and sew down the side, across the bottom, and up the other side.

SEW THE LINING TOGETHER

1. Pin the 2 lining 9″ × 11″ pieces right sides together.

2. Sew the sides and base together, leaving a 4″ opening for turning along the base.

3. Pinch the base corners together and sew a 1″ gusset on both sides as you did with the exterior.

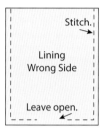

Sew the lining sides and base, leaving a 4″ opening at the base for turning.

FINISH THE BAG

1. Turn the lining right side out and insert inside the exterior. Line up the side seams and pin them together.

2. Sew around the top edge to join the lining and exterior together.

3. Turn the bag right side out through the opening in the lining base.

4. Push the lining inside exterior and press thoroughly.

5. Close the opening in the lining by topstitch on the machine or by hand with a ladder stitch.

6. Use a buttonhole foot to sew a buttonhole onto the flap. Sew your button to the front exterior.

7. Slide the tri-glide slide onto the long strap and set it in place with the rectangle ring.

Make It Your Own

- Dress up the bag by adding a leather accent or leather strap.

- Use canvas or heavier fabric and reduce the amount of interfacing to save time and provide a different texture.

- Add some cute wings, ears, and so on for an animal-themed bag.

- Add more pockets to the lining for extra organizing possibilities.

- Experiment with different sizes—you can make this really simple and smaller or larger with more zippers.

SIMPLE CLASSIC WALLET

Finished size: *8″ × 4½″*

Every woman needs a pretty wallet to keep herself organized. Handmade wallets are special since you can use your skill with color and print combinations to make something unique. This wallet is made using cotton for easy washing, but try using canvas and accents of leather for something different. It's easy to make this project fit your own individual set of skills.

Supplies

Makes 1 wallet.

COTTON FABRIC

- **Fabric 1 (gray):** 1 fat quarter
- **Fabric 2 (yellow):** 1 fat quarter
- **Fabric 3 (cream):** 1 fat quarter

OTHER SUPPLIES

- **Midweight stabilizer:** 20″ wide, 1½ yards (such as Pellon 40)
- **Batting:** 1 piece 10″ × 8½″ for exterior
- **Nylon zipper:** 9″ long
- **Magnetic snap set:** ¾″
- **Needle and thread:** For hand sewing
- **Coordinating piping:** 20″ long
- **Heavy-duty sewing machine needle:** Size 100/16

Cutting

For making multiples of 3 wallets, refer to the fabric cutting guides (next page).

FABRIC 1 (GRAY)

- 1 piece 10″ × 8½″ for exterior
- 1 piece 7″ × 8½″ for large pocket
- 1 piece 5″ × 8½″ for credit card pocket
- 1 piece 5½″ × 8¼″ for flap

FABRIC 2 (YELLOW)

- 1 piece 7″ × 8½″ for large pocket
- 1 piece 5″ × 8½″ for credit card pocket
- 1 piece 5½″ × 8¼″ for flap
- 2 pieces 5″ × 8½″ for pocket lining
- 2 pieces 1″ × 5″ for zipper ends

FABRIC 3 (CREAM)

- 1 piece 10″ × 8½″ for interior
- 1 piece 5″ × 8½″ for credit card pocket

MIDWEIGHT STABILIZER

- 2 pieces 10″ × 8½″ for exterior and interior
- 2 pieces 3½″ × 8½″ for large pocket
- 3 pieces 2½″ × 8½″ for credit card pockets
- 2 pieces 5½″ × 8¼″ for flap

FABRICS USED: Chambray in Gray, Yellow, and Cream from Andover Fabrics

Fabric 1:

8.5″ × 10″	8.5″ × 5″	8.5″ × 10″	8.25″ × 5.5″	8.5″ × 10″
	8.5″ × 5″		8.25″ × 5.5″	
8.5″ × 7″	8.5″ × 5″	8.5″ × 7″	8.25″ × 5.5″	8.5″ × 7″

Fabric 1: 17″ × 42½″

Fabric 2:

8.5″ × 5″	8.5″ × 5″	8.5″ × 5″	8.25″ × 5.5″	8.5″ × 5″
8.5″ × 5″	8.5″ × 5″	8.5″ × 5″	8.25″ × 5.5″	8.5″ × 5″
8.5″ × 7″	8.5″ × 5″	8.5″ × 7″	8.25″ × 5.5″	8.5″ × 7″

Fabric 2: 17″ × 42½″

Fabric 3:

8.5″ × 10″	8.5″ × 10″	8.5″ × 10″
8.5″ × 5″	8.5″ × 5″	8.5″ × 5″

Fabric 3: 15″ × 30″

Fabric cutting guides for making 3 wallets

Construction

Seam allowances are ¼″ unless otherwise noted.

MAKE THE FLAP

1. Cut curved corners on all the flap pieces, using the Simple Classic Wallet flap pattern (pullout page P2).

2. Layer stabilizer behind the exterior and interior flap pieces and baste around the edges.

3. Stitch piping on the 3 curved sides of the exterior flap piece, keeping the raw edges aligned.

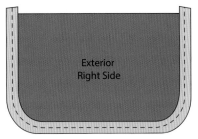

Topstitch the piping onto the flap.

4. Sew the exterior and interior flap pieces right sides together on the 3 curved sides, using the stitches from the piping as the guide. Turn right side out and press flat.

5. Mark the center of the interior side with a pin about ¾″ from the piping. Insert the flat half of the magnetic snap through the interior fabric and 1 layer of stabilizer.

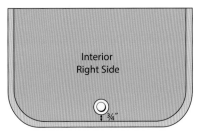

After you have turned the piece right side out, insert the flat side of magnetic snap.

6. Baste the top raw edge closed.

MAKE THE EXTERIOR

1. Layer stabilizer and batting below the wrong side of the 10″ × 8½″ exterior piece. Baste the 3 pieces together around the edges.

2. Center the flap on one of the 8½″ ends (the flap should be about ⅜″–½″ smaller on either side), with exterior fabrics facing. Baste the layers together.

3. Attach the other half of the magnetic snap to the base end of the exterior (opposite the end with the flap), centered 4″ from the edge and through the exterior fabric, stabilizer, and batting.

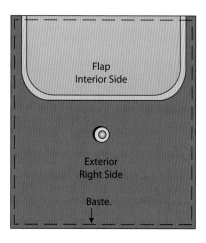

CREDIT CARD POCKETS

1. Fold and press the 5″ × 8½″ pockets pieces in half, wrong sides together, making them 2½″ × 8½″.

2. Open and insert 2½″ × 8½″ stabilizer in between the folds.

3. Topstitch the folded edge on all 3 pockets.

4. Zigzag stitch the raw edges of the pockets closed.

5. Fold the interior piece in half widthwise and finger-press to mark the center. Layer an 8½″ × 10″ piece of stabilizer underneath the interior piece.

6. Arrange the credit card pockets and place the first pocket 1″ from the base of the interior piece. Pin it in place and sew across the raw edge base to attach to the interior piece.

7. Place the next credit card pocket ½″ from the base, pin it in place, and sew across the raw edge. Place the final credit card pocket flush with the base of interior piece, pin it in place, and sew it across the raw edge of the pocket piece.

8. Use chalk or a water- or air-soluble marker to mark the vertical center of the pockets. Set your machine to a ¼″ zigzag stitch and sew the line to divide the pockets in half.

LARGE POCKETS

1. Fold and press the 7″ × 8½″ pockets pieces in half, wrong sides together, making them 3½″ × 8½″.

2. Open and insert 3½″ × 8½″ stabilizer in between the folds.

3. Decide which pocket will be in front of the other. Take this chosen folded piece, unfold it, and sew it right sides together, making a tube. The stabilizer should be caught by the stitches on one side. Turn the piece right side out and press flat.

4. Topstitch along the folded edge of both pockets and zigzag stitch the base of the pocket that will be in the back.

5. Measure ¾″ up from center fold you finger-pressed in Credit Card Pockets,

Step 1 (previous page). Pin and sew the back pocket in place.

6. Then measure ½″ up from the center fold and pin the front pocket in place. Topstitch it in place ¼″ from the bottom folded edge of the pocket.

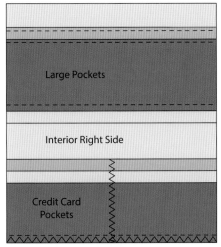

Sew all the pockets in place with a zigzag stitch (to reduce bulk) except for the front large pocket.

7. Baste all 5 pockets in place along outside edge of the interior piece to keep everything in place.

ZIPPER AND ZIPPER LINING

1. Open the zipper halfway. Cut the zipper down to 8″ total by cutting equally off the ends. This removes the stoppers on either side. Leave the zipper pull in the center.

2. Press the 1″ × 5″ zipper ends in half to make each one 1″ × 2½″. Open and press one end under ½″ toward the inside fold. Repeat with the other end. The pieces should now measure 1″ × 1½″.

3. Sandwich the zipper between the folded ends of the zipper end pieces and sew them in place ⅛″ from the edge. Do this for both ends of the zipper. For the separated end of the zipper, use pins to hold the ends in place.

Attach the folded zipper ends.

4. Switch over to the zipper foot on your machine. Center the zipper on the top edge of the interior piece above the large pockets, with the right side of the zipper facing the right side of the interior. Sew the zipper in place using the zipper foot.

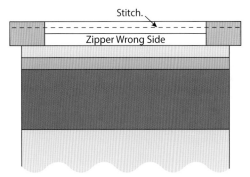

Attach the zipper to the interior.

5. Wait to sew the exterior onto the other right side of the zipper until last. Instead, sew the 2 pocket lining pieces with right sides facing onto the wrong side of the zipper. Use the stitches from sewing the interior to guide you on one side and then use the zipper foot to guide you when sewing the other side of the pocket lining onto the back side of the zipper.

6. To sew the exterior onto the other front side of the zipper, place the zipper right side down on the exterior, sandwiching the flap that was basted to the exterior earlier. Pin in place and use the stitches from attaching the lining to the wrong side of the zipper to guide you when sewing the exterior to the zipper.

SIDES AND POCKET LINING

1. Make sure the zipper is halfway open. Separate the pocket lining from the exterior and interior of the wallet.

2. Pin the corners of the exterior and interior with right sides together. Also pin the corners of the pocket linings. The seams of the zipper should be pinned down toward the pocket lining. Pin around the whole piece to hold the layers in place.

3. Because it is thick around the zipper section, switch over to a heavy-duty needle. Leave a 5″ opening in the base of the pocket lining and sew around the rest of the piece.

4. Clip the corners and turn the piece right side out through the opening in the pocket lining. Check to make sure all the seams look good. Press the pocket opening under to match the existing seam. Hand sew the opening closed with a ladder stitch (see Cross Your Heart Bag, Finish the Bag, Step 5, page 64).

5. Push the pocket into the zipper and close the zipper. Press the entire piece thoroughly. Test the magnetic snap to make sure it is a good fit.

6. Topstitch starting ½″ below the zipper, down one side, across the bottom, and up the other side. Stop ½″ from the zipper and backstitch.

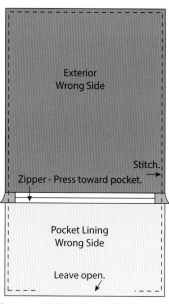

Sew around the wallet and lining.

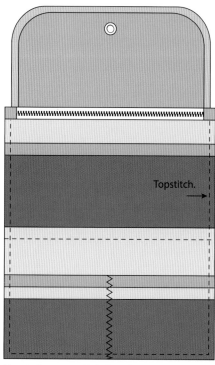

Topstitch starting ½″ below the zipper.

--- *Make It Your Own* ---

- Eliminate the zipper pocket to make it faster— some people prefer to carry a separate change purse anyway.

- Offer to monogram or personalize the flap of the wallet to make it extra special for customers who like that look.

- If you are a good at combining fabrics, use a variety of fabrics for each pocket and piece—people love the mix.

COORDINATION *Queen*

Although many of us can sew and make beautiful creations, there are some who have the special gift of mixing fabrics beautifully. You know who you are! You see a project and just know how to make it unique and special with your fabric choices and personal style. In running a handmade business, if this is your talent, please let it shine. This section features projects you can use to show off your mixing-and-matching skills.

DOLLY WITH STYLE

Finished size: 7″ × 17″

SUGGESTED PRICE POINT

$30 TO $42

There is nothing sweeter or more nostalgic than a handmade dolly. All children should have them and it just might be your job to be the creator. It is easy to put your own style to work on this pattern—change the hair, the clothes, and the face—customize them for your special clients. It's time to put your talents to the test. Customers will pay quite a bit for a beautifully handcrafted doll so extra details and fine quality materials do matter. My customers really appreciate that I use a tan fabric for the body that looks more like their children than the traditional white muslin.

Supplies

Makes 1 doll.

COTTON FABRIC

- **Fabric 1 (solid color):** 1 fat quarter

- **Fabric 2 (prints):** 1 or 2 prints to total 1 fat quarter

OTHER FABRIC

- **Knit or wool felt fabric:** 1 fat quarter

- **Wool felt:** 1 piece 7″ × 14″

OTHER SUPPLIES

- **Elastic:** ⅜″ wide, 10″ long

- **Polyester fiberfill**

- **Embroidery hoop:** 10″ × 10″

- **Embroidery floss and needle**

Cutting

FABRIC 1 (SOLID COLOR)

- 2 pieces 7″ × 7″ fabric for head

- 4 pieces 2½″ × 6½″ for legs

- 4 pieces 2″ × 6″ for arms

FABRIC 2 (PRINTS)

- 2 pieces 6″ × 7″ for body

- 1 piece 7″ × 18″ for skirt

WOOL FELT

- 2 pieces 7″ × 7″ for hair

Construction

Seam allowances are ¼″ unless otherwise noted.

MAKE THE ARMS AND LEGS

1. Cut out all pieces of the dolly using the Dolly with Style pattern pieces (pullout page P1), except the front head piece.

2. Sew together 2 arm pieces, right sides together, but leave the top end open. Turn it right side out and press flat. Stuff half full with polyester fiberfill and then push the fill all the way to the bottom. Baste the top closed. Repeat with the other arm pieces.

3. Repeat Step 2 with the leg pieces. Again, push the batting down to the bottom and baste closed.

FABRICS USED: Mojave in Illuminated and Windmarks in Mirage from the Tule collection by Leah Duncan for Art Gallery Fabrics

MAKE THE HAIR AND HEAD

1. Trace the outline and features of the face onto the face fabric, but don't cut it out yet.

Put the fabric into an embroidery hoop and embroider the face using your favorite techniques. After the embroidery is finished, cut out the face.

2. Sew the hair onto the front and back head pieces with coordinating thread. Follow the markings on the front hair pattern piece to make a part in the hair, using thread for extra texture.

3. Sew the front head and a body piece right sides together. Press the seams down toward the body. Repeat with back head and back body piece.

ATTACH THE ARMS AND LEGS

1. Position the legs and arms on the front body, facing in toward the center. Pin and sew ⅛″ from the raw edges.

Sew the arms and legs to the body.

2. Place the back of the dolly right sides together with front of the dolly, sandwiching the legs and arms. Pin, then sew the pieces together leaving a 3½″ opening between the legs.

FINISH THE DOLL BODY

1. Turn the body right side out and stuff with polyester fiberfill. Make sure you get the stuffing all the way up to the head so it is nice and full.

2. Hand sew the opening closed with a ladder stitch (see Cross Your Heart Bag, Finish the Bag, Step 5, page 64).

3. Roll the arms and legs between your fingers to redistribute the filling and "fluff" out the arms and legs.

MAKE THE SKIRT

1. Sew the short edges of the skirt piece right sides together to make a loop.

2. Serge or zigzag stitch the top raw edge of the skirt. Press the top edge over toward the wrong side ½″. Sew the fold down ⅛″ from the edge to make a casing. Leave a 1″ opening.

3. Fold the bottom edge under toward the wrong side ¼″ and press. Then fold again ½″ and press. Sew ⅛″ from the first folded edge to make the hem.

4. Use a bodkin or safety pin attached to one end of the ⅜″ elastic. Slide the elastic through the opening and pull it through the casing. When it is all the way through, pin the ends of the elastic together and try the skirt on your dolly.

5. When you're sure the skirt is a good fit , sew the ends of the elastic together. Topstitch the opening in the casing closed.

Try the skirt on your dolly.

Make It Your Own

- Make yarn hair for your dollies instead of using felt.

- Lengthen the arm pattern piece by ½″. Make a hand by cutting 1½″ from the rounded tip. Use printed fabric for the arm and solid fabric (that matches the face) for the hand. Sew right sides together and press seam toward the arm.

- Make boy dolls by leaving off the skirt and changing the hair.

- Use gray felt for hair and make granny and grandpa dolls. Lots of grandparents buy dolls for their grandchildren.

- Paint the face if that is your talent.

- Offer custom dolls to your customers. Have them send in hair color, skin color, eye color, and so on.

- Add rosy cheeks with a pink crayon and freckles with a fine-tip fabric marker.

- Have fun adding trim to the skirt and neckline.

BIG BOXY PATCHWORK BAG

Finished size: 17˝ wide × 17˝ high × 5˝ deep

More Sewing to Sell—Take Your Handmade Business to the Next Level

Using a mix of fabrics is a great way to use up leftovers from other projects. Look for combos that look fabulous together without putting in too much effort to make everything match perfectly. It's the perfect opportunity to give your work the style that your customers will love—you know what they want … go for it and have fun.

Supplies

Makes 1 bag.

COTTON FABRIC

- **Assorted fabrics:**
  10 different pieces, each at least 9″ × 9″ (*Note:* If desired, you can choose 10 squares from a precut 10″ × 10″ square pack.)

- **Fabric 1 (cream):** 1⅜ yards

- **Fabric 2 (handle):** ⅜ yard

OTHER SUPPLIES

- **Fusible fleece:** 45″ wide, ¾ yard (one-sided, such as Fusible Warm Fleece 1 by The Warm Company)

- **Midweight stabilizer:** 20″ wide, 1¾ yards (such as Pellon 40)

- **Midweight fusible interfacing:** 20″ wide, ½ yard (such as Pellon 931TD)

- **Magnetic snap set:** ¾″

Cutting

ASSORTED FABRICS

From 10 different pieces:

- 8 squares 9″ × 9″ for exterior

- 2 pieces 9″ × 5″ for side pockets

FABRIC 1 (CREAM)

- 1 piece 22″ × 5″ for base

- 2 pieces 15″ × 5″ for sides

- 2 pieces 17½″ × 17½″ for lining

- 2 pieces 5″ × 26½″ for lining sides/base

- 1 piece 9″ × 18″ for lining pocket

FABRIC 2 (HANDLE)

- 2 pieces 5″ × 22″ for handles

FUSIBLE FLEECE

- 2 pieces 17″ × 17″ for exterior front and back

- 1 piece 5″ × 22″ for exterior base

- 2 pieces 15″ × 5″ for exterior sides

- 2 pieces 2¼″ × 21″ for handles

MIDWEIGHT STABILIZER

- 2 pieces 17½″ × 17½″ for lining front and back

- 1 piece 5″ × 52″ for lining sides
  (*Note:* Cut 3 strips 5″ × 20″ and assemble into 1 long strip; then cut to 5″ × 52″.)

MIDWEIGHT FUSIBLE INTERFACING

- 2 pieces 8¼″ × 5″ for exterior side pockets

- 1 piece 9″ × 9″ for lining pocket

FABRICS USED: Floral Retrospective collection by Anna Maria Horner for FreeSpirit Fabrics

Construction

All seam allowances are ¼″ unless otherwise noted.

SEW THE EXTERIOR PATCHWORK

1. Sew 4 of the 9″ × 9″ squares right sides together to make a large square. Press the seams open. Fuse 17″ × 17″ fleece to wrong side of the patchwork, centered. The patchwork should be about ¼″ larger on all sides.

2. Quilt the piece to your liking. I did a simple outline of the seams to make it quick and easy.

3. Repeat with the other 4 squares and the other 17″ × 17″ piece of the fusible fleece.

MAKE THE HANDLES

1. Press the short ends of the handle ½″ toward the wrong side of the fabric.

2. Press the long side of the handle wrong sides together so it measures 2½″ × 22.

3. Open up the fabric and press fusible fleece to one side, lined up with the crease made in Step 2 and between the end creases.

4. Press the raw edges under ¼″ on both long sides. Sew around the perimeter of the handle ⅛″ from the edge. Fold back together with the center crease and press.

5. Measure and mark 3½″ from each end and pin the folded handle between the marks.

Sew the handle closed ⅛″ from the edge, stopping and starting 3½″ from each end.

Fold the handle in half and sew 3½″ from either end.

6. Press the ends of the handle flat. Pin one side of the handle onto the front exterior 4″ from the left side and 2½″ down from the top edge. Pin the other end of the handle 4″ from the right side and 2½″ down from the top edge.

7. Topstitch a 2″ × 2″ square to attach the handle. Then, topstitch from one corner diagonally to the opposite corner. Repeat with the other side of the box to create an X. Repeat for the other handle attachments.

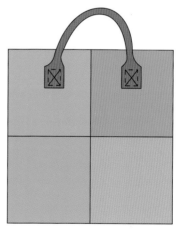

Sew handles onto the front and back.

SEW THE BASE AND SIDES

1. Fuse fleece to the wrong side of the 5″ × 22″ base piece. Quilt to your liking.

2. Press the top edge of the 5″ × 9″ pocket piece toward the wrong side ¼″ and then again ⅜″. Open the pressed folds and fuse interfacing below the bottom fold and to the base of the fabric on the wrong side. This will reduce bulk on the side pockets.

Finally, fold the pressed fabric back down over the interfacing and topstitch ¼″ from the top of the pocket.

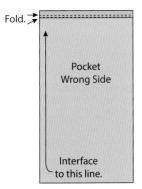

Fuse the interfacing below the folds.

3. Fuse fleece to the wrong sides of the 5″ × 15″ side pieces.

4. Line up the pocket with the bottom edge of the side piece and baste it in place. Repeat Steps 1–3 to make a pocket for the other side piece.

5. With right sides together, sew the side pieces to either 5″ end of the quilted base piece. Press the seams toward the base piece and topstitch on the base side.

ASSEMBLE THE EXTERIOR

1. Mark the center edge of the base/side piece with a water- or air-soluble marker or a pin. Pin the center of the base to the center bottom seam of the patchwork, right sides together. Then pin the base to both corner edges also. Continue to pin up the sides until the base/side is pinned to the front. Sew in place. At the corner, stop with the needle down, lift the presser foot, and adjust the fabric. Continue sewing.

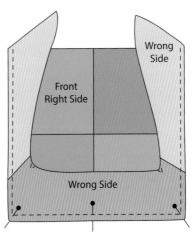

Sew the base/side piece to the front.

2. Pin and sew the back to the other side of the base/side piece.

3. The side pieces should be about ½″ longer than the front pieces. Trim away any excess.

MAKE THE LINING POCKET

1. Press the 9″ × 18″ piece in half, wrong sides together, to make a 9″ × 9″ piece. Open back up and fuse interfacing to one half.

2. Pin the piece right sides together and sew around the 3 raw edges, leaving a 3″ opening on one side.

3. Turn the piece right side out, gently poke out the corners, and press thoroughly.

4. Topstitch across the folded edge.

5. Layer a matching piece of stabilizer behind each 17½″ × 17½″ lining piece and baste ⅛″ from the edge all the way around.

6. Pin the pocket onto one of the 17½″ × 17½″ lining pieces, centered between the sides and 4″ from the base.

7. Sew in place around the sides and bottom of the pocket.

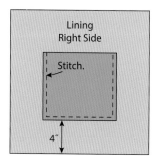

Center the pocket on the lining and sew it in place.

MAKE THE LINING

1. Sew the 2 lining side pieces 5″ × 26½″, right sides together, to make one long piece that measures 5″ × 52½″. Press the seam open.

2. Baste the lining pieces to the coordinating stabilizer pieces ⅛″ from each edge.

3. Mark the bottom center of the 17½″ × 17½″ pieces. Use the center seam from the long piece in Step 1 and pin right sides together around the bottom and sides, just as you did with the exterior pieces.

4. Sew both 17½″ × 17½″ pieces to the long base/side piece, right sides together, leaving a 5″ opening on one of the base sides for turning.

5. Attach the magnetic snap centered on each front piece 1½″ from the top edge on both sides of the 17½″ × 17½″ pieces. You can add an extra 2″ square of stabilizer or interfacing behind each snap for reinforcement, if you wish.

SEW THE LINING AND EXTERIOR TOGETHER

1. Turn the exterior right side out. Insert the exterior inside the lining.

2. Pin at the 4 seams that attach the sides and the front and back of the exterior and lining. Then pin around the rest of the bag top, pushing the handles inside between the exterior and lining.

3. Sew all the way around the top edge.

4. Turn the bag right side out through the side opening in the lining. Push the lining inside the exterior and press thoroughly.

5. Topstitch the lining opening closed.

6. Topstitch around the top of the bag to finish. Handles should be moved out of the way to stitch around the top.

Make It Your Own

- You don't have to use the 9″ × 9″ blocks—use half-square triangles, smaller squares, or any other pattern to add interest. Just make sure the exterior pieces are 17½″ × 17½″ when you are done piecing.

- Fussy cutting a really cute print and framing it with coordinating fabrics can add a lot of interest to your bag.

- Change up the size to make it more rectangular or smaller according to your tastes.

QUICK STRING LAP QUILT

Finished size: 50˝ × 70˝

I love making quilts, but I don't want to spend so much time on one that I price myself out of selling it reasonably. They are an investment in time and resources. What if you could make a lovely quilt but save time making it so you could sell it and feel good about the price? This string quilt project is for you—it takes some time, but not as much as the traditional method. Be sure that all the fabric you use is similar in weight.

If you're worried that you might make a quilt that may not sell, keep in mind that a beautiful quilt makes a fantastic backdrop for your show booth if you have one. Price it at what it is worth, and until the right buyer comes along, use it as an enticing prop to bring in customers. They will see your skills and want to buy something smaller.

Supplies

Makes 1 quilt.

COTTON FABRIC

- **Fabric 1 (white or cream):** 1⅝ yards
- **Fabric 2 (gray):** 1 yard
- **Fabric 3 (orange):** 1 yard
- **Fabric 4 (teal):** 1 yard
- **Fabric 5 (yellow):** 1 yard
- **Backing:** 3⅛ yards
- **Binding:** ⅝ yard

OTHER SUPPLIES

- **Batting:** 1 piece 56˝ × 76˝
- **¼˝ foot:** For your sewing machine

Cutting

FABRIC 1 (WHITE OR CREAM)

- 20 pieces 2½˝ × 38˝

FABRIC 2 (GRAY)

- 3 pieces 5½˝ × 38˝
- 3 pieces 4½˝ × 38˝

FABRIC 3 (ORANGE)

- 3 pieces 5½˝ × 38˝
- 3 pieces 4½˝ × 38˝

FABRIC 4 (TEAL)

- 3 pieces 5½˝ × 38˝
- 3 pieces 4½˝ × 38˝

FABRIC 5 (YELLOW)

- 3 pieces 5½˝ × 38˝
- 3 pieces 4½˝ × 38˝

BINDING

- 7 strips 2¼˝ × WOF

FABRICS USED: Scallop Dot in Graphite, Tangerine, Opal, and Corn from the Chroma Basics collection by Rae Ritchie for Dear Stella; and Kona Cotton in White from Robert Kaufman Fabrics

Construction

Seam allowances are ¼″ unless otherwise noted. Accurate seam allowances are very important in creating quilt squares that fit together!

ASSEMBLE THE QUILT TOP

1. You will sew the strips in the following order:

    a. 5½″-wide gray

    b. 2½″-wide white or cream

    c. 4½″-wide orange

    d. 2½″-wide white or cream

    e. 4½″-wide teal

    f. 2½″-wide white or cream

    g. 5½″-wide yellow

2. Once all 7 pieces are sewn together, press all the seams open. Turn it over and press the right side also. Trim the piece to 36″. It should measure 36″ × 24½″.

3. Repeat this process 5 more times to make a total of 6 pieces, alternating the contrast pieces between the 4½″ and the 5½″ to give variety. You will have 2 extra white strips.

4. Trim the pieces down to 36″ wide.

5. Along the one short side, mark the center of each white strip with a pencil or water- or air-soluble marker. Then mark 45° angles up toward the top and then crisscross across the entire piece as shown (above right). Be careful to cut the same way to make 8 squares with the white down the center. Each block will be 8½″ × 8½″ square—check your consistency by using your ruler and measuring 8½″ between diagonal lines.

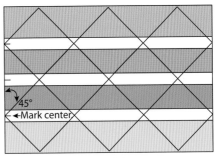

Cut as accurately as possible!

6. Take the 4 large triangles from the top and bottom that are left over, and sew them on either side of a 2½″ white strip of fabric. Trim them down to 8½″ × 8½″.

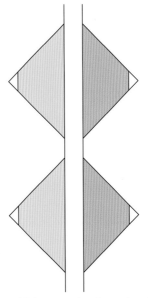

Add the extra triangles to the white strip.

7. Repeat Steps 5 and 6 with the other 5 sections. This will give you a total of 60 squares.

8. Arrange the squares 6 across and 10 down. You can arrange them either in a diamond pattern or X's.

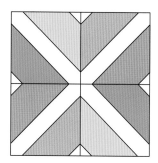

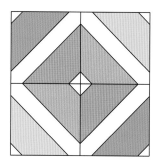

9. Sew the blocks together in the order you choose to create the quilt top. Press the seams open.

FINISH THE QUILT

1. Piece the backing. Spread it out and tape or pin it down. Place the batting on top, and then the quilt top.

2. Baste with needle and thread or pins.

3. Quilt as you choose.

4. Trim away the extra batting and backing.

5. Bind using your favorite method.

Make It Your Own

- Use the scraps from cutting the squares for a fun, scrappy, modern quilt backing.

- Use colors that reflect your style.

- Go for a more scrappy look by using fabric leftover from other projects.

EASY DOES IT APRON

Finished size: 24″ × 35″

SUGGESTED
PRICE POINT
$24 TO **$36**

A classic well-designed apron is the foundation for so many pretty variations. You can add ruffles, mix fabrics, and experiment with embellishments and appliqué. Play with the pocket to make the apron unique to your style and business vision. A high-quality fabric goes a long way in the quest for the perfect apron. This one is made using Tinted Denim from Cloud9 Fabrics, and it is fabulous. Also, the style of the ties makes this version adjustable to a variety of sizes.

Supplies

Makes 1 apron.

COTTON FABRIC

- **Fabric 1 (yellow denim, canvas, or chambray):** 1 yard

- **Fabric 2 (pink):** 1 fat quarter for pocket (*Note:* This can be quilting cotton or denim, canvas, or chambray.)

- **Fabric 3 (print):** ¼ yard for straps (*Note:* I recommend quilting cotton.)

OTHER SUPPLIES

- **Tube turner**

Cutting

FABRIC 1 (YELLOW DENIM, CANVAS, OR CHAMBRAY)

- 1 piece 26″ × 36″ for body

- 2 pieces 4″ × 7″ for tabs

FABRIC 2 (PINK)

- 15″ × 10″ for pocket

FABRIC 3 (PRINT)

- 2 strips 2½″ × WOF for straps

Construction

Seam allowances are ¼″ unless otherwise noted.

SEW THE APRON BODY

1. Fold the body fabric wrong sides together so that it measures 13″ × 36″. Use the Easy Does It Apron pattern (pullout page P1) to shape the top portion of the apron.

2. Topstitch the curves ⅝″ from the edge. Then press the raw edges ¼″ toward the wrong side. Fold under another ⅜″ and press. The second pressing should easily fold under along the topstitching. Press the curves again and then topstitch ¼″ from the outside folded edges.

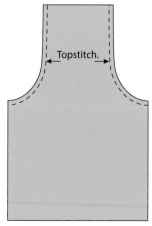

Stitching along the curve before you press makes for easy curved hemming.

To Make Multiples

Most denims, chambray, and canvas come in 54″–60″ widths, allowing you to easily make two aprons from 1 yard of fabric. To make two aprons from a 42″-wide quilting cotton, you would need to narrow the width of the apron to 20″, making them more ideal for kid's aprons.

FABRIC USED: Tinted Denim from Cloud9 Fabrics

3. Press the top edge under ¼″ toward the wrong side. Then press under again ¾″. Leave this for a moment while you sew the straps.

4. Sew the 2½″ × WOF pieces of fabric rights sides together to make long tubes. Turn the tubes right side out with a tube turner or a large safety pin. Tuck one end inside the tubes for a finished edge and press the piece thoroughly.

5. Topstitch along both long sides and the folded-under edge of each strap.

6. Slide the raw ends of the straps under the folded and pressed top edge where the top and the curves connect. The straps will hang down the wrong side of the apron at this point. Sew the fold down and over the straps

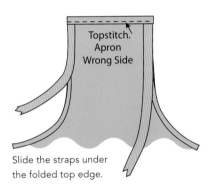

Slide the straps under the folded top edge.

7. Fold the straps up toward the top edge and topstitch the top edge of the fold and the strap in place.

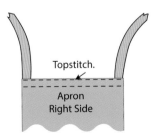

MAKE THE TABS

1. Fold the 4″ × 7″ pieces right sides together so they are 2″ × 7″. Sew the raw edges and press the seam half open. To do this, with the seam on the edge of your ironing board, open one side of the seam and press flat toward the center. This will make it easier to press when you do the next step.

2. Turn right side out and press flat with the seam down the middle of one side.

3. Fold in half with the seam inside the fold to make a 3½″ loop and press.

SEW THE SIDE AND BOTTOM SEAMS

1. Fold the side seams and bottom edge ¼″ toward the wrong side. Press.

2. Press the sides again, this time ⅜″. Insert the loops where the curve meets the side seam underneath the folds. Pin them in place.

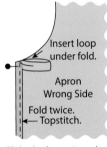

Slide the loops into the side hems.

3. Topstitch the side seam and then fold the loop over toward the edge. Sew the loop in place to hold it. Press.

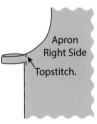

4. The bottom edge is already folded over ¼″; fold it again ¾″ toward the wrong side. Press and topstitch it in place.

MAKE THE POCKET

1. Fold and press one 15″ edge of the pocket piece ¼″ toward the wrong side. Then press around the other 3 sides ¼″. Fold and press the top edge ⅜″ and topstitch it in place.

2. Center the pocket on the apron so it is 5¼″ from each side and 2″ down from where the loop and the side curve meet. Pin.

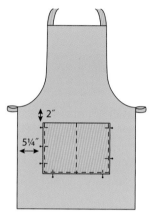

Pin the pocket.

3. Topstitch the pocket in place, leaving the top hemmed edge open.

4. Mark the vertical center of the pocket and sew a straight line to make a divider in the pocket.

FINISH THE APRON

Thread the left side strap through the right loop and the right side strap through the left loop. Tie the straps together behind the back.

Make It Your Own

- Use vintage sheets or fabric for a unique look. Make sure that it washes well, though.

- Use binding for the curved sides and around the bottom half to create more color.

- Use stencils or embroidery to write a fun message on your apron.

- Use 1″-wide cotton webbing for quick straps instead of sewing your own.

Trendsetter

Do you love to follow the latest fashions and trends? Do you find yourself being the first of your friends trying out new designs and clothing styles? If so, choosing your sewing projects to showcase these talents can be a *big* advantage for your handmade business. Even if you have a more traditional style, adding some fun, easy, trendy pieces to your shop can help boost sales and grab attention. The following projects can be altered to show the latest styles, colors, and designs.

FOLD-OVER MINI CLUTCH

Finished size: 8″ × 10″

Giving your pieces a little leather accent can really attract customers and take your handmade shop to a more sophisticated level. This little clutch is fun because of its versatility and simple construction. It can be presented as a fold over or you could add some interfacing and sell it as a unique zipper pouch. Although a plastic zipper would work fine, the weight of the brass zipper helps the top to fold down nicely and looks great with the modern look of the clutch.

Supplies

Makes 1 clutch.

FABRICS

- **Cotton fabric:** 1 fat quarter

- **Denim or canvas:** 1 fat quarter or 1 piece 18″ × 22″

- **Leather, suede, or kraft-tex (by C&T Publishing):** 1 piece 7″ × 10″

OTHER SUPPLIES

- **Brass/jeans zipper:** 7″ long

- **Swivel hook and D-ring:** ½″

- **Craft or bulldog clips:**
  To hold leather or kraft-tex together (*Note:* kraft-tex can't be pinned.)

- **Leather needle:**
  For your sewing machine

- **Leather and zipper feet:**
  For your sewing machine

To Make Multiples

To make four clutches, you'll need ½ yard of exterior fabric, ½ yard of lining fabric, and a 14″ × 20″ piece of leather, suede, or kraft-tex.

TIP: *kraft-tex: Kraft Paper Fabric*
C&T's kraft-tex is a great substitute for leather—it's less expensive, can be washed and dried, is easy to sew, comes in a variety of colors, and is vegan-friendly for those who want to avoid leather.

Cutting

COTTON

- 2 pieces 5″ × 10″ for exterior top

- 1 piece 2″ × 14″ for strap

- 1 piece 2″ × 4″ for strap loop

DENIM OR CANVAS

- 2 pieces 8″ × 10″ for lining

LEATHER, SUEDE, OR KRAFT-TEX

- 2 pieces 3½″ × 10″

FABRICS USED: Camping Floral White from the Trail Mix collection by Rae Ritchie for Dear Stella

Construction

Seam allowances are ¼″ unless otherwise noted.

MAKE THE EXTERIOR

1. Change the needle on your machine to the leather needle.

2. Sew the 5″ × 10″ fabric and 3½″ × 10″ leather right sides together. Use clips instead of pins to hold the pieces together. Using a pressing cloth and working on the fabric side, press the seam toward the leather.

3. Topstitch on the leather side ⅛″ from the seam.

4. Repeat with the other exterior side.

5. Place the exterior in front of you on your worktable with the fabric side facing up. Measure in 1½″ from the side on the top edge. Mark and use a ruler to cut a diagonal line down to the base. Repeat with the other side.

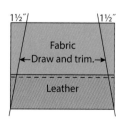

Shape the exterior sides.

6. Cut the same diagonal lines on the other exterior piece.

ADD THE D-RING TO THE SIDE

1. Press the 2″ × 4″ piece of cotton fabric in half, wrong sides together, to make it 4″ × 1″.

2. Open up the pressed fabric and press the raw edges in toward the center fold. Fold it in half again so that the piece measures ½″ × 4″.

3. Topstitch both 4″ edges.

4. Thread the D-ring to the center of the fabric strap. Fold in half with the D-ring in the center. Use the zipper foot to sew across the strap close to the D-ring.

5. Measure 4″ up from the base of one exterior. Baste the D-ring strap in place facing in toward the center of the piece and parallel to the seamline below. Because the side of the exterior piece has been cut at an angle, the raw edge of the strap will hang over the edge of the exterior piece at the top; you can trim it to follow the slant.

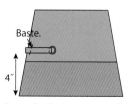

Baste the D-ring on one of the exterior pieces.

ADD THE ZIPPER

1. Center and pin the zipper right sides together with one top exterior piece. Sew them together using a zipper foot.

2. Pin and sew the other side of the zipper to the top of the other exterior piece.

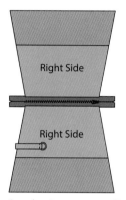

Sew the zipper centered between the 2 exterior pieces.

MAKE THE LINING

1. Cut the 8″ × 10″ lining pieces with the same diagonal as the exterior pieces.

2. Sew the right side of the lining pieces to the wrong side of the zipper sides, using the previous seamline as a guide.

3. Repeat with other lining side and other zipper side.

4. Pull the lining pieces away from the exterior pieces and pin the corners right sides together. Pin the sides and bottom of the lining together as well.

5. Pull the exterior sides together and use a clip to hold the bottom corners right sides together. Clip the side and bottom right sides together also. Pin the zipper seam toward the exterior.

6. Starting at the base of the lining, about 3″ from the side edge, sew toward the edge and then up the side, over the zipper seam, down the side of the exterior, and all the way around to about 3″ from the other side of the lining base. This will leave a 4″ gap in the base of the lining side.

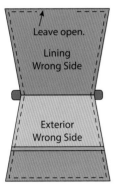

Sew around the perimeter of both the lining and exterior.

FINISH THE CLUTCH

1. Turn the piece right side out through the opening in the lining. Check your seams and then press the opening in the lining under toward the wrong side to match the seams.

2. Sew the opening closed with a ladder stitch (see Cross Your Heart Bag, Finish the Bag, Step 5, page 64) or topstitch it closed ⅛″ from the edge.

3. Press carefully and use a pressing cloth over the leather.

MAKE THE WRIST STRAP

1. Press the 2″ × 14″ piece of cotton in half, wrong sides together, to make it 1″ × 14″. Open and press the raw edges in toward the center fold. Fold the piece back together by the center fold so the folded piece is ½″ × 14″. Do not stitch this yet.

2. Thread the swivel clip to the center of the folded piece.

3. Open the just the ends of the folded piece a few inches. Then, without twisting the piece, sew the ends right sides together.

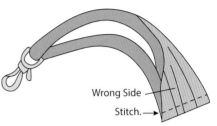

Sew the ends of the strap together.

4. Finger-press the seam open and then fold the edges back together. Press the piece again so the seam is flat.

5. Topstitch both edges of the strap loop, moving the swivel hook out of the way as you sew around.

6. Topstitch both sides of the strap together ½″ above the hook to hold it in place. Use a zipper foot if needed to get close to the swivel hook hardware.

Make It Your Own

- Use suede or even high-quality wool felt instead of leather for the bottom exterior.
- Adjust the size to 10″ × 12½″ or even 12½″ × 15″ for a larger piece.
- Add a chain shoulder strap and use black shiny leather for a cute evening clutch.

HAND-PRINTED PILLOW

Finished size: 14″ × 28″

SUGGESTED
PRICE POINT
$38 TO **$50**

Designed and made by Sarah Case

Customers are looking for something unique and beautiful when they are purchasing something handmade. This beautiful hand-printed pillow by Sarah Case is the perfect example of how to really wow your customers. Use your special talents with color combinations and design to create a gorgeous handmade pillow.

For more great ideas, see the book *Transfer Embellish Stitch—16 Textile Projects for the Modern Maker* by Jen Fox and Sarah Case (from C&T Publishing).

Supplies

Makes 1 pillow.

COTTON FABRIC

- **Any color:** 1 yard total

OTHER SUPPLIES

- **Premade piping or cording:** 2⅝ yards
- **Pillow form:** 14″ × 28″
- **Quilter's template plastic:** For plastic stencil. Or use other type of translucent plastic sheet.
- **Fine-tip permanent marker**
- **Craft knife**
- **Cutting mat**
- **Jacquard deColourant:** Color remover, available online and in art supply stores.
- **Foam craft brush**
- **Repositionable spray adhesive**
- **Embroidery floss**
- **Embroidery needle**

Cutting

COTTON

- 1 rectangle 15″ × 29″ for pillow front
- 2 rectangles 15″ × 19″ for pillow back

Construction

Seam allowances are ¼″ unless otherwise noted.

MAKE THE PILLOW FRONT FABRIC

1. Make a plastic stencil, using the Hand-Printed Pillow stencil pattern (pullout page P1).

2. Use a repositionable spray adhesive on the back of the plastic stencil to minimize seepage and adhere the stencil to the right side of the pillow front.

3. Use deColourant (see Using deColourant, page 96) and the stencil to create the design: Referring to the project photo (previous page), begin applying the deColourant in the center. Wipe the stencil between every couple motifs to remove any deColourant that has gotten onto to the wrong side of the stencil. Work out from the center until the design is complete.

4. Once the fabric is dry and has been ironed, embellish the design as shown or as desired, using a running stitch or another embroidery stitch of your choice. Secure the beginning and end of each length of stitches with a small knot on the wrong side of the fabric.

FABRIC USED: Kona Cotton in Pacific Blue from Robert Kaufman Fabrics

Using deColourant

Jacquard deColourant (formerly called Discharge Paste) is used to remove areas of color from natural-fiber fabrics. The color revealed is a surprise! Be sure to do a test with your fabric before starting the project so you know what to expect.

1. Cover your work surface with plastic. With a foam craft brush, apply the deColourant to the fabric through your stencil. Use a dabbing motion to ensure saturation with minimal bleeding beyond the designated areas. Let the fabric dry (or use an iron to speed up the drying time) and remove the stencil.

2. Iron, with steam, on a setting that correlates to your fabric. This step releases the color; keep ironing until the color stops releasing or you like the color that you have.

SEW THE PILLOW TOGETHER

1. Pin the piping to the perimeter of the right side of the pillow front fabric, keeping the raw edges aligned. Clip the piping seam allowance at the corners as needed to allow it to round the corners.

Clip the corners of the piping.

2. To join the piping ends, overlap by 1½˝, open the seam and cut the cording out of one end, place the corded end inside the now-uncorded end, and fold the raw edge of the uncorded end under. Pin in place.

3. Use a zipper foot to sew the piping around the perimeter of the pillow front.

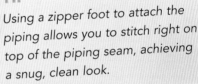

TIP

Using a zipper foot to attach the piping allows you to stitch right on top of the piping seam, achieving a snug, clean look.

4. On one pillow back piece, fold over a 15˝ edge ½˝ toward the wrong side and press. Fold over another ½˝ and press again. Stitch close to the edge of the inner fold. Repeat this step with the other pillow back piece.

Fold the edges of the pillow backs.

5. Layer the pillow front and back pieces, right sides together, aligning the raw edges all around so that the finished edges of the back pieces overlap in the center. Pin in place and sew around the raw edges. Clip the corners. Turn the pillow cover right side out and press if necessary.

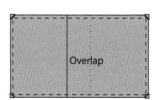

Overlap

Layer the pillow backs on the pillow front.

6. Insert the pillow form.

Make It Your Own

- This simple stencil is an example of how to create a pillow in this style. Use your talents to create your own stencil and use Sarah's techniques to achieve the look you want.

- Play with the size of the pillow. For example, a 16˝ × 16˝ pillow form is a common shape and if you create your own stencil, it might appeal more to your customers.

BEST-SELLING HEADBAND

Finished size: 3″ × 20″

SUGGESTED
PRICE POINT
$9 TO **$18**

This knit fabric headband is as basic and beginner a project as any out there! But many a sewing business has been created from the lowly headband. This version starts with the basic and then shows you several variations to make it more interesting. Choose nice high-quality knit fabric that is easy to work with, wears well, and will make your simple headband look fabulous. The small amount of fabric that the headband uses will make investing in high-quality fabric well worth it and improve your sales.

Supplies and Cutting

Makes 1 headband.

- **Cotton knit fabric:** 1 piece 6″ × 20″ (*Note:* Make sure you cut the fabric in the direction that stretches the most.)

- **Needle and thread:** For hand sewing. Or use Light Steam-A-Seam 2 (¼″ tape, by The Warm Company).

To Make Multiples

Knit fabric usually comes at least 40″ wide and often as wide as 60″. From 1 yard of fabric, you can make 12 of the basic headband and narrow base headband.

Construction

Seam allowances are ¼″ unless otherwise noted.

MAKE THE BASIC HEADBAND

1. Fold the cut fabric in half lengthwise right sides together so that the piece is 3″ × 20″.

2. Measure 1½″ from the top edge and then, using the stretch stitch setting on your machine, sew the raw edges together. Stop 1½″ from the other end.

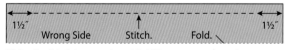

Make the fabric into a tube with 1½″ open at each end.

3. With the seam on the edge in front of you, open one side of the seam and press flat toward the center. Pressing one side of the seam open will make the seam easier to flatten when you turn it right sides out.

4. Turn the piece right side out and press flat with the seam running down the center, not the edge. Press the 1½″ ends under toward the wrong side to match the seam.

Position the seam down the center of one side.

FABRICS USED: Wink Knit in Pond, Duck, and Orange from Birch Organic Fabrics

5. Loop the ends together to meet right sides together on the side of the piece that does not have the seam. Pin the raw edges together. Open up the ends of the tube so that the ends meet all the way across the 6˝.

6. Sew the ends together slowly, stopping and adjusting the fabric as needed.

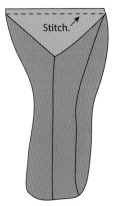

Sew the ends of the tube together.

7. With your fingers, open the seam you just made and then fold the edges of the tube back in place. The pressing from Step 4 should bring them back together neatly. Press again.

8. Use coordinating thread and hand sew the opening closed though just the seam side layer with a small ladder stitch (see Cross Your Heart Bag, Finish the Bag, Step 5, page 64).

9. Press again and you are finished.

ALTERNATIVE LOOKS

Off-Center Knot

1. Increase the size of the fabric to 6˝ × 22½˝ and follow Make the Basic Headband, Steps 1–4 (previous page). Tie a knot a few inches off center. Make sure that the knot does not flip the piece around and that the seam sides are still facing down.

2. Press the knot and then close the headband up, following Make the Basic Headband, Steps 5–9 (at left).

Narrow Base

1. Fold the 6˝ × 20˝ piece in half horizontally. Then fold in half vertically. The piece should now be 11˝ × 3˝. Mark 4˝ from the edge and then make a diagonal cut with your scissors toward the edge 1½˝ down from the top.

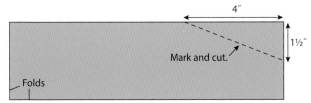

To narrow the ends, make cuts from the short ends that angle toward the center.

2. Make the rest of the headband as described in Make the Basic Headband, Steps 1–9 (previous page).

Double Headband with Fancy Knot

1. Cut 2 pieces 3˝ × 23˝, instead of 1 piece 6˝ × 20˝.

2. Sew each into a tube as described in Make the Basic Headband, Steps 1–4 (page 98), and leave the 1½˝ ends open.

3. Turn the tubes right side out with a tube turner (or use your favorite turning method) and press them flat.

4. Tie the fancy knot (double-carrick bend) as shown, choosing to make it centered or slightly off center for a different look.

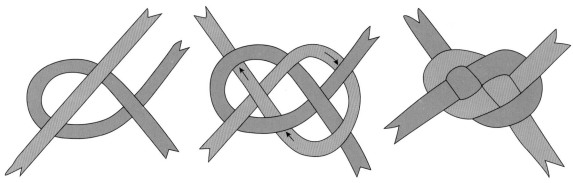

This classic fisherman knot, or *double-carrick bend*, looks great on a headband.

5. Adjust the knot to make it as even as possible. Press it flat.

6. Sew the ends together following Make the Basic Headband, Steps 5–9 (page 99).

Make It Your Own

- Extend the length and width, and use a soft, lightweight knit fabric for a very pretty cowl.

- Sell in sets of 3 in coordinating colors for a gorgeous gift.

- Extend the length even further and braid 3 pieces together.

BIG TRENDY TOTE

Finished size: 20″ × 14″

A big tote is always useful and customers are always looking for something fun to carry everything around in. This bag has a unique casual design that buyers love and a simple easy construction that you will love! Also, your budget will love that it uses two half-yards of fabric with almost no waste. Be sure to experiment with the handles to get the look you want.

Supplies

Makes 1 tote.

COTTON FABRIC

- **Fabric 1 (stripe print):** ½ yard for exterior
- **Fabric 2 (floral print):** ½ yard for lining
- **Fabric 3 (navy duck cloth or canvas):** 1 fat quarter for base

OTHER SUPPLIES

- **Midweight fusible interfacing:** 20″ wide, 1¼ yards (such as Pellon 931TD)
- **Twisted cotton rope:** ½″ thick, 40″ long for handle
- **Duct tape:** 1 piece 2″ × 3″
- **Cream-colored cotton fabric:** 1 piece 2½″ × 5″ (*Note:* Try to match the rope color.)
- **Button:** 1″ diameter
- **Elastic cording:** ⅛″ wide, 4″ long

Cutting

Refer to the fabric cutting guides (below) for the best use of fabric.

FABRIC 1 (STRIPE PRINT)

- 2 pieces 12″ × 18″ (cut vertically) for exterior front and back
- 2 pieces 9″ × 15″ (cut horizontally) for exterior sides
- 2 pieces 3″ × 9″ (cut vertically) for exterior handle casing

FABRIC 2 (FLORAL PRINT)

- 2 pieces 12″ × 18″ for lining front
- 2 pieces 9″ × 15″ for lining sides

FABRIC 3 (NAVY DUCK CLOTH OR CANVAS)

- 2 pieces 12″ × 18″ for exterior and lining base

MIDWEIGHT FUSIBLE INTERFACING

- 2 pieces 12″ × 18″ for exterior front pieces
- 2 pieces 9″ × 15″ for exterior sides

| Exterior Front 12″ × 18″ | Exterior Front 12″ × 18″ | Exterior Side 9″ × 15″ | Handle Casing 3″ × 9″ |
| | | Exterior Side 9″ × 15″ | Handle Casing 3″ × 9″ |

Exterior cutting guide

| Lining Front 12″ × 18″ | Lining Front 12″ × 18″ | Lining Side 9″ × 15″ | Waste |
| | | Lining Side 9″ × 15″ | |

Lining cutting guide

FABRICS USED: Blue Waves from the Ramble & Roost collection by Betsy Olmsted for Clothworks

Construction

Seam allowances are ¼˝ unless otherwise noted.

To Make Multiples

If you are making more than one tote, this bag fits nicely onto half-yard cuts of fabric.

MAKE THE EXTERIOR

1. Fuse interfacing to the wrong side of the exterior cotton pieces.

2. Sew the 12˝ × 18˝ front and back pieces to the 18˝ edges of the 12˝ × 18˝ duck cloth base piece, right sides together. Press the seam up toward the front and back exterior pieces. Topstitch across the exterior right side ⅛˝ from the seam.

3. Fold the side exterior in half, right sides together, so that it measures 4½˝ × 15˝. Mark 1˝ from the folded edge and then up 3˝ along the folded edge. Cut a right triangle between these 2 marks to make a dart. While still folded, cut slight curves on the base corners.

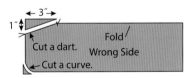

Cut a dart on the fold and curve the corners.

4. Sew the dart right sides together.

5. Mark the center of the duck cloth exterior piece from

Step 2. Pin the seam of the dart to the center mark on the duck cloth. Pin the side piece and the exterior front. Back and base right sides together.

6. Sew the sides and exterior front, back and base together. Repeat with the other side exterior piece.

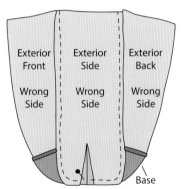

Match the dart and the center of the duck cloth base and stitch.

7. Press each 3˝ raw edge of the 3˝ × 9˝ casing pieces under ½˝ toward the wrong side of the fabric and sew it in place.

8. Press one 9˝ edge of each casing piece (now 8˝ because the sides are pressed under) under ¼˝ toward the wrong side.

9. Line up the raw edge of the casing with the top raw edge of the side exterior. Center the

casing between the seams and sew across the folded bottom edge to attach to the side exterior.

ADD THE ELASTIC CORDING

Mark the center top of the exterior back. Fold the 4˝ cording in half. Sew the cord in place on the right side of the fabric, with the loop facing down toward the center of the piece. Sew back and forth in the seam allowance a few times to secure.

MAKE THE LINING

Repeat Make the Exterior, Steps 2–6, to make the lining. The only change is that you need to leave a 5˝ opening in a side seam to turn the piece right side out.

ATTACH THE LINING AND EXTERIOR

1. Turn the exterior right ride out and insert into the lining so the pieces are now right sides together.

2. Pin first at the side seams and then around the top edges of the lining and exterior.

3. Sew around the entire top edge.

4. Turn the piece right side out through the opening in the side seam of the lining.

5. Press the opening raw edges toward the wrong side of the lining, and then topstitch the opening closed with ⅛″ seam allowance. Alternatively, hand sew the opening closed with a ladder stitch (see Cross Your Heart Bag, Finish the Bag, Step 5, page 64).

6. Push the lining inside the exterior and then press the bag, paying special attention to the top seam.

7. Topstitch ¼″ from the top edge between the 2 side casings, not all the way around.

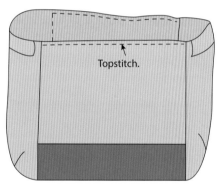

Topstitch just between the casings.

ADD THE HANDLE

1. Thread the length of rope through both casings.

2. Hold the ends of the rope together so they are flush. Duct tape them together so they are secure.

3. Fold the piece of 2½″ × 6″ fabric in half right sides together so it measures 2½″ × 3″. Sew it right sides together around the 3 open sides but leave a 1″ opening for turning.

4. Turn the piece right sides out, gently poke out the corners, and press flat.

5. Wrap the cotton piece tightly around the duck cloth section of the handle. Hand sew closed with a ladder stitch.

Fabric cover for duct tape

6. Adjust the rope handle so the covered duct tape is inside one of the casings.

7. Sew the button to the exterior front, opposite the placement of the elastic cord.

Make It Your Own

- Make the width of the bag smaller, perhaps to 8″, add interfacing to the lining and a magnetic snap to make the bag structured more like a purse.

- Show off your skills and crochet a handle.

- Use different fabrics for the side pieces for a different look.

ENVIRONMENTALLY *Conscious*

As you already know, people shopping handmade are not looking to save money—they are looking for value in the form of high-quality, original, artisan work from makers they want to support. These types of people are often also conscious of sustainability. They want to feel good on many levels about their purchases—buying local, buying organic materials, or buying something that has been recycled. If this type of sewing appeals to you, you are in luck. The market is great for environmentally conscious sewists, so be sure to take advantage.

ON-THE-ANGLE LAPTOP BAG

SUGGESTED
PRICE POINT

$32 TO **$45**

Finished size: 16″ × 11″ × 1″

So many people carry their laptops around with them all the time, wanting to work wherever they are. Making a stylish bag for the tech lovers is a great way to boost your business. The off-center fold-over of this bag adds style and doubles as at flap to help protect the precious cargo. You will enjoy making this almost as much as the buyer will enjoy carrying it. My sizing is for a standard 15″ × 10″ × 1″ laptop; but I suggest offering your customer custom sizing, since changing proportions a little will not affect the look of the bag very much, and they'll get exactly what they need.

Supplies

Makes 1 bag.

COTTON FABRIC

- **Fabric 1 (seafoam green):** ½ yard for exterior

- **Fabric 2 (flax):** ½ yard for lining

- **Fabric 3 (denim):** 1 fat quarter or 1 piece 18″ × 22″ for flap

OTHER SUPPLIES

- **Midweight fusible interfacing:** 20″ wide, 1¼ yards (such as Pellon 931TD)

- **Fusible fleece:** 45″ wide, ½ yard (one-sided, such as Fusible Warm Fleece 1 by The Warm Company)

- **Magnetic snap set:** ¾″

- **Midweight cotton webbing:** 1″ wide, 1 piece 6″ long and 1 piece 54″ long

- **Rectangle rings:** 1″ size, 2 rings

- **Adjustable slide buckle:** 1″ size

- **Tassel cap**

- **Double-capped brass rivets and rivet tool:** (I use the ones by Dritz.)

Cutting

For the best use of fabric, refer to the interfacing cutting guide (below).

FABRIC 1 (SEAFOAM GREEN)

- 2 pieces 17″ × 12½″ for exterior

FABRIC 2 (FLAX)

- 2 pieces 17″ × 12½″ for lining

FABRIC 3 (DENIM)

- 2 pieces 16″ × 9″ for flap

MIDWEIGHT FUSIBLE INTERFACING

- 2 pieces 17″ × 12½″ for lining

- 2 pieces 16″ × 9″ for flap

FUSIBLE FLEECE

- 2 pieces 17″ × 12½″

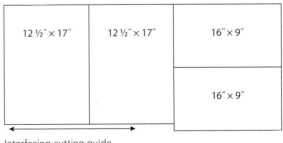

Interfacing cutting guide

To Make Multiples

If you are making more than one bag, this bag fits nicely into half-yard pieces of fabric.

FABRICS USED: Essex Yarn Dyed fabrics in Denim, Flax, and Seafoam from Robert Kaufman Fabrics

Construction

Seam allowances are ¼˝ unless otherwise noted.

MAKE THE EXTERIOR

1. Fuse the fusible fleece to the wrong side of both exterior 17˝ × 12½˝ pieces.

2. Sew the pieces right sides together down the 12½˝ sides and across the bottom.

3. Pinch the bottom corners together to flatten the seams between your fingers. Sew across 1˝ to create a gusset. Trim off the corner below the seam.

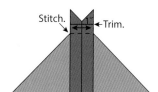

Pinch seams together to make a 1˝ gusset at the bottom of the exterior.

4. Turn the exterior right side out and press.

ATTACH THE HANDLES

1. Loop the 6˝ piece of webbing through both rectangle rings. Fold the strap in half with the rings in the middle and use the zipper foot to sew close to the rings and secure them in place.

2. Baste the loop centered over the seam between the exterior front and back at the top of one side of the bag.

3. Baste the other piece of webbing centered over the side seam at the top of the other side of the bag.

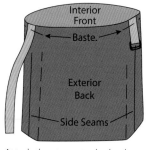

Attach the straps to the back exterior.

MAKE THE FLAP

1. Fuse interfacing to wrong side of both 17˝ × 9˝ flap pieces.

2. Use the On-the-Angle Laptop Bag pattern (pullout page P1) to cut the flap angles.

3. Sew the flap pieces, right sides together, down the sides and across the angled bottom.

4. Trim the corners and turn the piece right side out. Press thoroughly.

5. Topstitch down the sides and along the angled bottom ¼˝ from the edge.

6. Install the flat side of the magnetic snap at the angled corner on the flap lining side.

Install the snap.

7. Pin the flap to the back side of the exterior, on top of the straps, with the exterior side of the flap facing the right side of the exterior body. Baste the top raw edges together with a ⅛˝ seam allowance,

8. Flip the flap up and over to fold naturally over the front exterior, allowing for 1˝–1½˝ of thickness once the bag has a laptop inside. Then, mark the spot where the snap on the flap hits the exterior front. Install the other, larger half of the snap in this spot.

MAKE THE LINING

1. Fuse interfacing to the wrong sides of the 17″ × 12½″ lining pieces.

2. Sew the pieces, right sides together, down the sides and across the bottom. Leave a 5″ opening on the bottom for turning.

3. Pinch together the bottom corners and make a 1″ gusset (see Make the Exterior, Step 3, previous page).

SEW THE EXTERIOR AND LINING TOGETHER

Insert the exterior inside the lining so that right sides are facing. Pin at the side seams and sew the top edges together.

FINISH THE BAG

1. Turn the bag right side out through the opening in the lining.

2. Press the lining opening raw edges under to match the seam. Topstitch or hand sew the opening closed.

3. Push the lining inside the exterior and press thoroughly.

4. Finish the strap with the adjustable slide buckle. Pull the strap through the outer bars of the buckle and then loop it through the double rings on the other side of the bag. Then wrap the loose end of the strap around the center bar of the buckle and stitch to hold it in place.

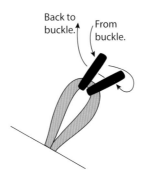
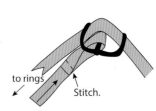

Loop the strap through the double rings.

Wrap the strap around the adjustable buckle.

ADD THE OPTIONAL TASSEL

1. Create a tassel with a tassel maker, using your favorite method. Use the tassel cap to secure the top of the tassel.

2. Secure the tassel chain to the end of the angled flap with a double-capped rivet, using a rivet tool.

- - - - - - - - - - *Make It Your Own* -

- Use different fabrics for all the pieces to add contrast.

- Experiment with canvas, waxed canvas, decor weight, and other fabrics to get a unique, sturdy look.

- Add a zipper to the opening to secure the laptop.

- If you don't like the angled flap, make a more traditional curved or rectangular flap.

- Use piping on both the flap and around the side and base seam for a fun contrast.

- Adjust the sizing:

    Laptop width + Laptop depth + 1″
    = Fabric width

    Laptop height + Laptop depth + 1″
    = Fabric height

EASY-LIVING BACKPACK

SUGGESTED
PRICE POINT
$32 TO **$45**

Finished size: 12″ × 15″ × 5″

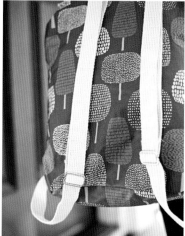

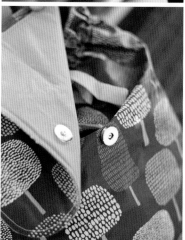

Backpacks can be made in so many ways. This version is casual and simple to make. You can showcase your favorite fabrics and sew up a pretty, practical bag that your customers will love. I used a lovely organic Matte Laminate from Cloud9 Fabrics for this bag. This size fits an average adult, but make one a little smaller and it is also perfect for kids. Backpacks are really popular right now, so be sure to take advantage of this fun trend.

Supplies

Makes 1 backpack.

COTTON FABRIC

- **Fabric 1 (print):** ½ yard
- **Fabric 2 (lining):** ½ yard
- **Fabric 3 (straps):** 1 fat quarter or scraps

OTHER SUPPLIES

- **Midweight fusible interfacing:** 20″ wide, 1½ yards (such as Pellon 931TD)
- **Fusible fleece:** 45″ wide, ¼ yard or 1 piece 9″ × 10″ (one-sided, such as Fusible Warm Fleece 1 by The Warm Company)
- **Rectangle rings:** 1″ size, 2 rings
- **Tri-glide slides:** 1″ size, 2 slides
- **Cotton webbing:** 2 pieces each 36″ long for straps
- **Magnetic snap set:** ¾″
- **Cording:** ¼″ wide, 2 pieces each 20″ long for drawstring
- **Zipper and buttonhole feet:** For your sewing machine

Cutting

FABRIC 1 (PRINT)

- 2 pieces 15″ × 16″ for exterior
- 1 piece 6″ × 10″ for base
- 1 piece 9″ × 10″ for flap exterior

FABRIC 2 (LINING)

- 1 piece 15″ × 22″ for lining front
- 1 piece 15″ × 10″ for lining back
- 1 piece 9″ × 10″ for lining flap

FABRIC 3 (STRAPS)

- 1 piece 2″ × 7″ for hanging strap
- 2 pieces 2½″ × 4″ for short straps

MIDWEIGHT FUSIBLE INTERFACING

- 1 piece 15″ × 22″ for lining front
- 2 pieces 15″ × 10″ for lining back
- 1 piece 9″ × 10″ for lining flap

FUSIBLE FLEECE

- 1 piece 9″ × 10″ for lining base

To Make Multiples

To make three, you'll need 1½ yards each of exterior fabric and lining fabric. Choose to use either lining or exterior fabric to make the hanging strap and short straps.

FABRIC USED: Matte Laminate in Glade from Cloud9 Fabrics

Construction

Seam allowances are ¼″ unless otherwise noted.

MAKE THE EXTERIOR

1. Pin the 36″ handles on either side of the 15″ × 16″ back exterior piece 1″ up from the bottom on the 15″ edges, facing in toward the center of the fabric. Baste them in place.

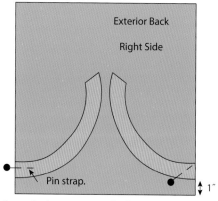

Exterior Back

Right Side

Pin strap.

1″

Baste the long straps to the front exterior piece.

2. Press the 2″ × 7″ hanging strap piece in half, wrong sides together, to measure 1″ × 7″. Open and then press the raw edges, wrong sides together, toward the center fold. Fold back together and press. It should now measure ½″ × 7″. Topstitch the open folded edges together.

3. Mark the center top of the back exterior piece. The center should be 8″ from the side edge. Flatten the ends of the 7″ piece together to make a loop. Pin the loop in place at the center of the back exterior with the loop pointing toward the middle of the back; baste in place.

4. Sew the 2½″ × 4″ pieces right sides together into tubes. Turn them right side out and press them flat with the seam down the middle. The tubes should now measure 1″ × 4″.

5. Loop one of the 1″ × 4″ pieces through a 1″ rectangle ring. Fold the strap in half with the ring inside and use the zipper foot to sew close to the ring to secure it in place. Repeat to make the second short strap.

6. Pin the short straps you just made on either side of the loop from Steps 2 and 3. Angle the pieces out toward the sides of the back about 30°. Baste.

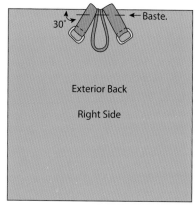

30° ← Baste.

Exterior Back

Right Side

Angle the short straps away from the center.

7. Sew the 2 exterior 15″ × 16″ pieces, right sides together, along the 15″ sides. Press the seams open.

ATTACH THE BASE
TO THE EXTERIOR

1. Mark the center bottom of the front and back pieces with chalk.

2. Change the stitch setting on your machine to the longest stitch. Sew along the bottom edge from one side seam to the other side seam. Do *not* backstitch and do *not* clip threads. Do the same between the other side seams on the bottom edge. This stitch is to ease the exterior fabric onto the base piece in the next step.

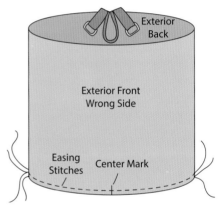

Easing the exterior to the base results in nice gathers around the corners and more space in the bag.

3. On the exterior base piece, make marks at the center of all 4 edges. Clip the corners to make them rounded.

4. Pin the exterior side seams to the marks on the 6″ sides of the base, right sides together. Pin below the easing stitch so it pulls easily in the next step. Then pin the center mark of the exterior front and back to the center marks on the front and back of the base piece.

5. Gently pull the threads from the ease stitch at the side seams. Pull enough so that they gather at the corners and fit perfectly with the base piece. Pin in place and sew all the way around the base.

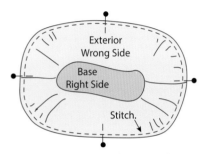

Gently pull the ease stitches to match the sides to the base.

MAKE BUTTONHOLES FOR THE DRAWSTRING

1. Turn the piece right side out. Mark the front top edge center. Measure down 1˝. Make 2 vertical lines 1˝ long with chalk or a water- or air-soluble marker ½˝ on either side of this center mark. Fuse a 2˝ × 2˝ piece of scrap interfacing to the wrong side of the fabric behind these marks.

2. Use your buttonhole foot to stitch 1˝ buttonholes on these 2 marks. Use a seam ripper to open the buttonholes. Clip any loose threads.

3. Measure down 6½˝ from that top center mark and install the thick half of the magnetic snap.

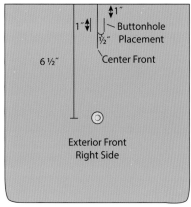

Buttonhole and snap placement

MAKE THE FLAP

1. Fuse interfacing to the wrong side of the lining flap piece. Layer the lining and exterior flap pieces together and cut a curve at the 2 bottom corners using the Easy-Living Backpack curve-cutting pattern (pullout page P2).

2. Pin and sew the flap exterior and lining, right sides together, leaving the straight top edge open. Notch the seam allowance along the curve.

3. Turn right side out and press flat. Topstitch the flap down the sides and across the bottom.

4. Install the other half of the magnetic snap 1˝ from the center bottom of the flap.

5. Baste the flap to the back of the exterior, exterior sides facing, sandwiching the rectangle ring pieces and hanging strap.

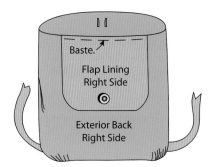

Baste the flap to the back exterior.

MAKE THE LINING

1. Fuse interfacing to the wrong side of the 10″ × 15″ lining piece. Then fuse another layer of interfacing to the same piece so that you have a double thickness.

2. Fuse interfacing to the wrong side of the 15″ × 22″ lining piece.

3. Pin and sew the 2 lining pieces right sides together up the 15″ sides only. Leave a 1″ gap ½″ from the top edge on both sides. This will be for adding the drawstring later. Also leave a 5″ gap on one side for turning.

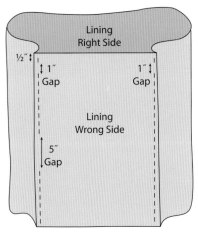

Sew up the sides of the lining.

4. Press the seams open. To prepare for sewing the lining sides to the base, mark the middle of the back lining piece—this is the smaller piece with double interfacing. Then mark the front center and the sides. Because the side seams aren't centered, use the center back as the guide for making the other marks. Sew ease stitches between the side marks as in Attach the Base to the Exterior, Step 2 (page 113).

5. Fuse fusible fleece to the wrong side of the lining base. Make the center marks on all 4 sides of the base. Trim the corners to curve as you did in Attach the Base to the Exterior, Step 3 (page 113).

6. Pin the lining sides and base right sides together at the center marks.

7. Gently pull the ease stitches. Pin and sew the lining and base lining together.

SEW THE LINING AND EXTERIOR TOGETHER

1. Turn the exterior right side out. Insert the exterior inside the lining with the back lining piece facing the flap on the exterior piece. Pin them together.

2. Sew the lining and exterior right sides together around the top.

3. Pull the piece right side out through the opening in the lining. Push the lining inside the exterior.

4. Press thoroughly and pay special attention to the top edge. Hand sew or topstitch the lining opening closed with a ⅛″ seam allowance.

5. Topstitch around the top edge. Topstitch over the short straps but keep the hanging strap out of the way along with the flap.

6. Using the base of one of the buttonholes as a starting point, sew straight back to where the back panel begins on the lining. On the lining side, this is where you left the 1″ gap. Repeat with the other side and the other buttonhole.

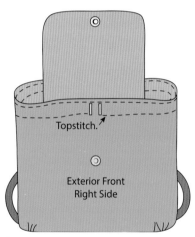

Sew a casing.

7. Use a sturdy safety pin or a bodkin and attach to the end of one of the drawstrings. Starting at the opening in the lining, pull the string through to the buttonhole opening on the exterior front. Leave a 1″ end at the lining opening. Tuck that end inside between the lining and the exterior and stitch it securely in place. Repeat with the second drawstring.

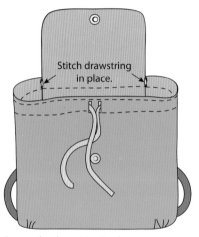

Secure the drawstring in place.

8. Pull the drawstrings and tie them in a bow. Close the flap and secure it to the magnetic snap on the exterior.

9. Slide the tri-glide slide onto the long strap and set it in place with the rectangle ring.

Make It Your Own

- Use piping on the flap and the exterior base.
- Use leather or suede on the flap to dress it up.
- Adjust the sizing to make it smaller for kids.

FOXY-BOXY TRAVEL DUFFLE

Finished size: 10″ × 12″ × 18″

A roomy duffle bag is a staple for everyone. This style is fun to make with the sturdy quilted base and the long easy handles. Your customers will love this unique take on the classic, and you will love making it quickly and giving it a lot of style. This duffle uses the length of a yard of fabric with some nice size scraps to easily use on another project such as the Cross Your Heart Bag (page 59), Simple Classic Wallet (page 65), or On-the-Angle Laptop Bag (page 106).

Supplies

Makes 1 duffle.

COTTON FABRIC

- **Fabric 1 (ticking stripe):** 1 yard for exterior top and interior pockets

- **Fabric 2 (rose-colored denim):** ⅔ yard for exterior bottom

OTHER FABRIC

- **Canvas or other heavyweight fabric:** 1⅜ yards for interior

OTHER SUPPLIES

- **Midweight fusible interfacing:** 20″ wide, 1¼ yards (such as Pellon 931TD)

- **Fusible fleece:** 45″ wide, ¾ yard (one-sided, such as Fusible Warm Fleece 1 by The Warm Company)

- **Nylon coil zipper or brass zipper:** 18″ long

- **Midweight cotton webbing:** 2 pieces 1½″ × 29″ for handles

- **Zipper foot:** For your sewing machine

Cutting

FABRIC 1 (TICKING STRIPE)

- 2 pieces 28″ × 10″ for exterior top

- 2 pieces 16″ × 16″ for lining pockets

FABRIC 2 (ROSE-COLORED DENIM)

- 1 piece 28″ × 25″ for base

CANVAS OR OTHER HEAVYWEIGHT FABRIC

- 2 pieces 28″ × 22¼″ for lining

MIDWEIGHT FUSIBLE INTERFACING

- 2 pieces 28″ × 10″

- 2 pieces 16″ × 8″ for lining pockets

FUSIBLE FLEECE

- 1 piece 28″ × 25″

FABRICS USED: Tinted Denim in Rose from Cloud9 Fabrics and vintage ticking stripe

Construction

Seam allowances are ¼″ unless otherwise noted.

MAKE THE EXTERIOR

1. Fuse interfacing to the back of both exterior top pieces.

2. Cut a 5″ × 5″ square from both top corners of both pieces. Discard the squares (or save for another project).

3. Measure 9″ in from one bottom side edge of the exterior top and mark with a water- or air-soluble pen. Pin the handle in place vertically from this location. Make sure it is straight, then sew up 5″ and across the handle and back down to the bottom edge. Loop the handle around and pin it to the other side 9″ in from the opposite edge. Sew as before. Repeat with the other handle and the other exterior top piece.

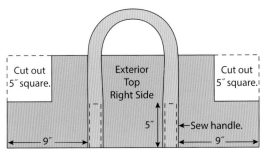

Place the handle and sew it in place.

4. Center the zipper on the top edge of one of the exterior top pieces, right sides together. Switch over to a zipper foot and sew the zipper to the exterior piece. Sew the other side of the zipper to the top edge of the other exterior top piece, right sides together.

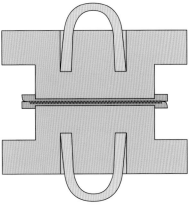

Sew the zipper right sides together with the exterior top.

5. Fuse fleece to the 28″ × 25″ base. Quilt as desired.

6. Find the center of each side (12½″ from the top edge) and cut out a rectangle that measures 5″ × 9½″. Do the same on the other side.

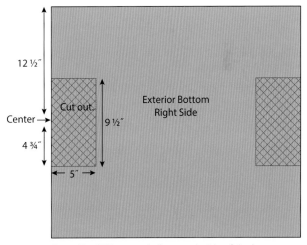

Cut a 5″ × 9½″ rectangle from each side of the base.

7. Sew the base to the top pieces, right sides together, matching the 28″ edges. Now it should be a loop. Press the seams toward the base and topstitch on the base side.

8. Sew the sides with right sides together, but leave the cutouts open.

MAKE THE LINING

1. Press the pocket piece in half wrong sides together to make a piece that measures 16″ × 8″. Fuse a 16″ × 8″ piece of interfacing to half of the piece. Then fold the piece in half, right sides together, and pin. Sew the 3 sides leaving a 4″ opening on the long bottom edge. Clip the corners and turn the pocket right side out. Gently push out the corners and iron flat, pressing in the seam allowances of the opening. Topstitch the top folded edge. Repeat with the other pocket piece.

2. Cut a 5″ × 5″ square from all 4 corners of the 2 lining 28″ × 22½″ pieces.

3. Pin the pocket pieces 6″ from the bottom and 6¼″ from the sides so that they are centered between the sides on the lining piece. Sew in place, leaving the top edge open. Mark and sew down the middle of the pocket to create a divider in each pocket.

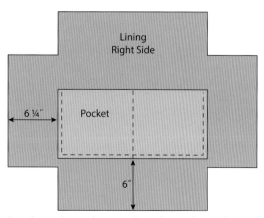

Sew the pocket as shown so that it fits nicely into the side of the duffle

SEW THE LINING AND EXTERIOR TOGETHER

1. Switch back to the zipper foot and attach the right side of the 2 lining pieces to the wrong side of the zipper, using the stitches of the exterior stitching as guides.

2. Switch back to a regular sewing foot and sew the bottom edges of the lining right sides together. Leave an 8″ opening for turning.

3. Sew the sides of the lining right sides together, leaving the 5″ × 5″ cutouts open.

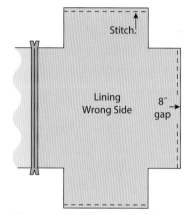

After sewing the zipper to the lining, sew the lining sides and base.

4. Working on the wrong side of the exterior fabric, fold the side seam up to meet the zipper seam. Work on the side that has the closed zipper ending (*not* the pull side). Pin on either side of the zipper to hold the fold in place.

5. Bring the wrong side of the lining side seam to meet the zipper seam. Use the pins from the last step to pin through both the lining and exterior materials and hold in place on either side of the zipper. Flatten out the opening on both the lining and the exterior and pin both layers together.

6. Sew across the layers and over the zipper (that is sandwiched between the exterior and lining) to make a boxy corner.

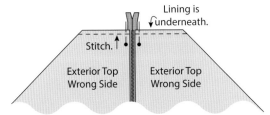

Hold the corners together to make a straight line. Pin, and then stitch.

7. Repeat this process with the other side of the zipper, but open the zipper about 8″ and then carefully pin the ends in place so they don't overlap and cause the zipper to close badly.

8. Flatten out the base corners on the exterior so that the center seams meet in the middle and the sides go out at a 45° angle. Sew them closed. Repeat this process on the lining. Now all the corners should be sewn.

FINISH THE DUFFLE

1. Pull the duffle right side out through the opening in the lining base and then through the zipper opening. Push the lining inside the exterior. Gently poke the corners out. Iron if needed.

2. Pull the lining out and press the opening raw edges under so they match the base seam. Topstitch or hand stitch the lining closed with a ladder stitch (see Cross Your Heart Bag, Finish the Bag, Step 5, page 64). Finished!

Make It Your Own

- Instead of cutting the 5″ × 5″ squares at the top, add swivel hook hardware and fold the edges down to hook onto D-rings on the side. This gives the customer extra room and looks great.

- Omit the quilting and use a sturdy canvas, duck cloth, or kraft-tex (page 91) for the base.

- Use patchwork to create a very unique and original look.

- Use just one fabric for the exterior and add leather handles with rivets.

- Increase or decrease the size for more options for your customers.

MARKET BAG

Finished size: 13″ × 13″ × 8½″

SUGGESTED
PRICE POINT
$12 TO **$18**

Reusable grocery bags are no longer something cute to bring along to the store if you happen to remember—they are now a staple for most people when doing their shopping—and durable, pretty, handmade totes are selling really well. This bag is great for your customer because it is sturdy, roomy, and folds up nicely. It is great for you because it uses two half-yards of fabric with almost no waste (depending on the width of your fabric) and the sewing is simple and quick. Using webbing for handles saves you more time and this bag has an optional panel of stiff fusible interfacing at the base for greater stability.

Supplies

Makes 1 bag.

COTTON FABRIC

- **Fabric 1 (exterior):** ½ yard*

- **Fabric 2 (lining):** ½ yard*

* If your fabric does not have 42″ of usable width, then ⅔ yard is required for both exterior and lining.

OTHER SUPPLIES

- **Midweight cotton or nylon webbing:** 2 pieces 1″ × 22″

- **Elastic:** ¾″ wide, 2 pieces each 6″ long

Optional:

- **Heavyweight fusible interfacing:** 1 piece 8½″ × 13½″ for sturdier base

- **Fray Check (by Dritz)**

Cutting

Refer to the fabric cutting guides (below) for the best use of fabric.

FABRIC 1 (EXTERIOR)

- 2 pieces 14″ × 18″

- 2 pieces 9″ × 13¾″

FABRIC 2 (LINING)

- 2 pieces 14″ × 18″

- 2 pieces 9″ × 13¾″

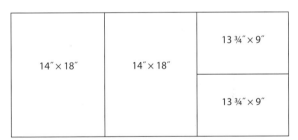

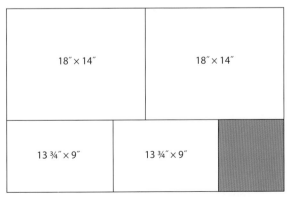

Cutting guides for exterior and lining

FABRICS USED: Organic Barkcloth Meridian Blue from Organic Cotton Plus

Construction

Seam allowances are ¼″ unless otherwise noted.

MAKE THE EXTERIOR

1. Sew the 14″ × 18″ pieces, right sides together, to make a piece that is 14″ × 35½″. Press the seam open.

2. Treat the ends of the handles with Fray Check or zigzag stitch the ends.

3. On one side, sew a handle 3″ from one edge of the 14″ side of the exterior piece. Repeat with the other side of the handle, attaching it 3″ from the other edge to form a loop that faces down toward the center seam. Attach the second handle the same way on the other 14″ edge of the exterior piece. This will be the front and back of the bag.

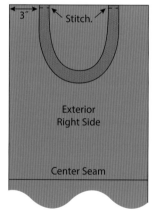

Sew handles to the front and back of the bag.

4. Mark the bottom center of the 9″ × 13¾″ side exterior piece, and pin it to the seam of the front and back piece, right sides together. Start sewing ¼″ from the edge of the side piece, then sew across the base and stop ¼″ from the other edge. Press the seam open.

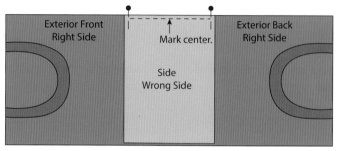

Sew the side bottom to the front and back.

5. Repeat with the other 9″ × 13¾″ piece on the other side of the front and back piece.

6. Fold the front piece up to line up with the top edge of a side piece and pin in place right sides together. Stitch. Press the seam open. Repeat with the back piece and the other side of the side piece

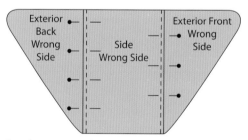

Sew the exterior side piece to the front and back.

7. Repeat with other side piece and the opposite edges of the front and back.

MAKE THE LINING

1. Sew the 14″ × 18″ lining pieces, right sides together, as in Make the Exterior, Step 1 (previous page).

2. Sew the bottom of the side lining pieces as in Make the Exterior, Steps 4–7 (previous page), but when sewing up the sides, stop 1½″ from the top and leave a 1″ opening, then stitch the last ½″. Repeat this on the 3 other sides. Leave a 4″ opening on one side seam for turning. Press the seams open.

SEW THE LINING AND EXTERIOR TOGETHER

1. Turn the exterior right side out and insert it inside the lining so they are right sides together. Line up the seams and pin them together.

2. Sew around the top edge to attach the lining and the exterior. When you get to a handle, backstitch to give the handle extra strength.

3. Turn the bag right side out through the opening in the lining.

4. Press the bag thoroughly and topstitch ¼″ from the top edge. On the sides only, topstitch 1¼″ from the top edge to create a casing for the elastic.

5. Using a bodkin or a safety pin, thread the elastic through the casing on the sides.

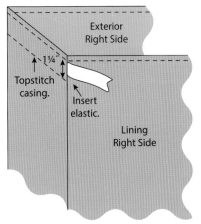

Thread the elastic through the casing on the sides.

6. After the elastic is pulled through, pin it on one side to secure it. Stitch it in place. Then pull the elastic all the way through so it gathers the side fabric and stitch it in place again, closing the opening in the side seam. Repeat with the other side of the bag.

7. Optionally, insert the 8½″ × 13½″ piece of heavy weight fusible interfacing in through the opening on the side you used for turning. The piece should fit snugly into the base of the bag between the exterior and lining layers. Stand the bag upright on your ironing board and insert the iron carefully inside the bag. Carefully fuse the interfacing to the base of the bag. Topstitch the opening on the side of the bag closed or sew by hand with a ladder stitch.

Make It Your Own

- For a quick-to-make tote, omit the base interfacing and topstitching the side seams.

- Make your own matching handles instead of using webbing.

- Use extra webbing to extend the handles all the way down the front of the exterior and meet at the base seam. To do this, make the handles 58″ long instead of 22″ long.

- Use interfacing to make this bag sturdier or use batting to give it a quilted look.

RESOURCES

Many of the listed companies will sell directly to you only if you meet their minimum purchase amounts. If you need smaller amounts of their products, their websites often list retail outlets.

FABRICS

Andover Fabrics
andoverfabrics.com

Art Gallery Fabrics
artgalleryfabrics.com

Birch Organic Fabrics
birchfabrics.com

Clothworks
clothworks.com

Cloud9 Fabrics
cloud9fabrics.com

Dear Stella
dearstelladesign.com

FreeSpirit Fabrics
freespiritfabric.com

Organic Cotton Plus
organiccottonplus.com

Robert Kaufman Fabrics
robertkaufman.com

OTHER SUPPLIES

The Buckle Guy
buckleguy.com

Clover
clover-usa.com

National Nonwovens
nationalnonwovens.com >
Products

Prym Consumer USA Inc.
prym-consumer-usa.com

Pellon
pellonprojects.com

The Warm Company
warmcompany.com

PHOTOGRAPHY

Shoot Fly Shoot
shootflyshoot.com

LBG Studios
Photography eBook:
lbgstudio.bigcartel.com >
Products > Photography for
Bloggers eBook

Etsy
*Seller Handbook
Photography series:*
etsy.com/seller-handbook >
Photography

CREATING YOUR OWN ONLINE SHOP

Big Cartel
bigcartel.com

E-junkie
e-junkie.com

Etsy
etsy.com

Shopify
shopify.com

MARKETING RESOURCES

**Market Your Creativity
by Lisa Jacobs**
marketyourcreativity.com

CreativeLive, Inc.
*Copywriting for Crafters,
online course by Lisa Jacobs:*
creativelive.com > search
Copywriting for Crafters

ABOUT THE AUTHOR

Virginia Lindsay is a self-taught sewist and lover all things fabric. She is the author of the popular sewing blog *Gingercake* and the designer behind the PDF pattern shop Gingercake Patterns (gingercake.bigcartel.com). She has designed 24 sewing patterns and has several published by Simplicity. She has done many craft shows and sews for her online shop (ginia18.etsy.com). Virginia has written two other sewing books, *Sewing to Sell—The Beginner's Guide to Starting a Craft Business* (by Stash Books) and *Pretty Birds* (by Running Press).

Virginia is the mother of four and is happily married to her husband, Travis. She lives outside of Pittsburgh in Freeport, Pennsylvania. Her kids inspire her every day and she spends a lot of time playing cards, watching soccer, throwing the baseball, and listening to piano practice. When she is not taking care of her big family, you will find her taking walks outside, vegetable gardening, and sewing away in her home sewing studio.

Visit Virginia online!
Website: gingercake.org

Also by
Virginia Lindsay

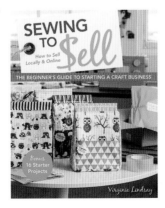

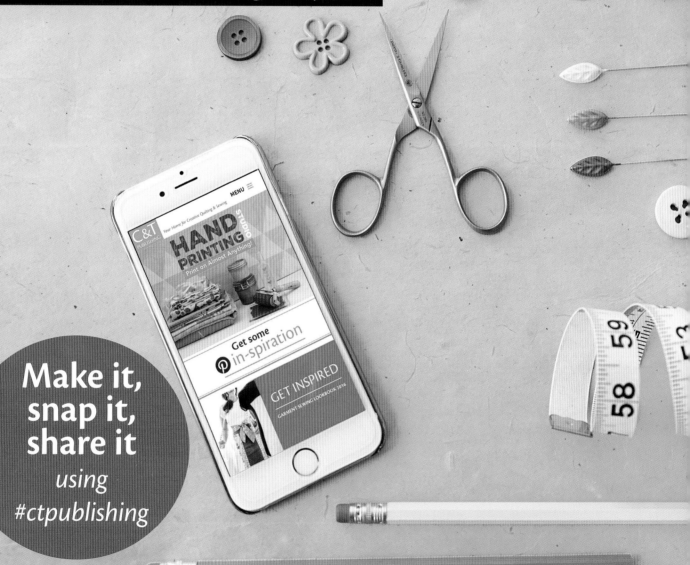

Want even more creative content?

Make it, snap it, share it *using* **#ctpublishing**